The Gift of Self

The Gift of Self

HEATHER WARD

Foreword by Kenneth Leech

Darton, Longman and Todd
London

First published in 1990 by
Darton, Longman and Todd Ltd
89 Lillie Road, London SW6 1UD

British Library Cataloguing in Publication Data

Ward, Heather
  The gift of self.
  1. Christian life
  I. Title
  248.4

  ISBN 0–232–51862–9

The window of the Transfiguration on the cover is
reproduced by courtesy of the Taizé Community, France
© Taizé, F-71250 Taizé Communauté

Phototypeset by Input Typesetting Ltd, London SW19 8DR
Printed and bound in Great Britain by
Courier International Ltd, Tiptree, Essex

Contents

Foreword by Kenneth Leech   vii

Acknowledgements   x

1 Who am I? – God and myself   1

2 The divided self   12

3 Becoming myself – a way of life   24

4 Selfhood, solidarity and intercession   41

5 The self that gives itself away   57

6 Narcissus at prayer? – the self and modern spirituality   67

7 The self in the Body of Christ – selfhood and community   82

8 Icon or idol? – the self in marriage and at work   98

References and further reading   116

Foreword

A true inwardness of spirit is a necessary component of that attainment of union and communion with God which is the goal of the Christian life. God is to be found within, at the heart, for he is, as Augustine and Julian of Norwich and so many others stressed, closer to us than we are to ourselves. God is the ground in which we stand. There can be no true spirituality without a return to the heart. And so the search for God has often been called the 'inner way' or 'the journey inwards'.

However, recent years have seen the disturbing growth in western Christianity of a cult of false inwardness, showing striking parallels to the gnostic and illuminist trends in earlier periods of Christian history. Attempts to 'internalize' the gospel are not new. But the recent growths have been particularly significant as a result of a combination of individualism – the legacy of the Reformation and the Enlightenment, a tradition strongly emphasized in current political ideology – and a notion of 'spirituality', itself a relatively modern word, as a private pursuit. Privatization began in the religious sphere, and so, as Marx pointed out, the criticism of religion is the beginning of all criticism. And so we find that much of contemporary spirituality is marked by a concern for self-awareness, self-realization, self-fulfilment. A whole industry of personal growth has developed, most of it having only the most tenuous relationship to orthodox Christianity. Indeed much of this movement separates internal growth from dogmatic belief of any kind – apart, that is, from unswerving and uncritical belief in the method and technique in question. Salvation by technique has a tendency to bring with it an element of fascism: this technique, and this technique only, will work.

Two aspects of current concern about the self are particularly dangerous. The first is a separation between inner and outer struggles and conflicts. Much current spirituality is world-denying and escapist. Spirituality becomes a way of becoming neutral, of turning aside from the complexity of the modern world and its demands. The second is a reduction of God to the self, a kind of theological narcissism. What comes to matter is self-improvement. God is incidental – as he was in classical gnosticism where what mattered was the spiritual technology which would promote knowledge and awareness. The individual becomes absorbed within the process of self-realization and self-discovery, and the gospel of God's transforming grace is reduced to a gospel of self-nurture. The American evangelical writer Jim Wallis has expressed it very well in many of his writings. Jesus comes into our lives to improve them, not to transform them. And it is always Jesus coming into *our* lives, whereas the thrust of the New Testament is that we are brought into *his* life.

Heather Ward's book is therefore particularly welcome. It is important, first of all, as a corrective and a warning against some really harmful reductionist trends in the present climate. For true spirituality is not concerned with the nurturing of the ego, but with its death through the self-emptying of *metanoia*, the total reversal which is the essential starting point of the Christian life. As Heather Ward says, 'True prayer marginalizes the ego by establishing God-in-himself at the centre of our being. Anything in prayer which works against this is inimical to the self, through fostering ego'. Feverish worry about our own growth is a sure sign of domination by the ego. The Christian call is to self-forgetfulness, self-abandonment, self-emptying. Here Dr Ward's warnings about the misuse of Myers-Briggs techniques and the Enneagram are extremely important.

This book is important, secondly, because it calls us back to the great tradition of Christian spirituality with its stress on transformation through incorporation into Christ. All the emphasis of the tradition is on God's grace in Christ, not on our personal spiritual development. Indeed there is virtually nothing about personal spiritual development in the New Testament: all the emphasis is on the New Creation, the Body of Christ, the Kingdom of God.

It is not surprising that among the influences on Heather Ward's thinking, the names of Irenaeus and F. D. Maurice appear throughout the text. The rediscovery of the Greek Fathers in the nineteenth century had major theological consequences, not least in the renewed emphasis on incarnation and atonement as the movement of humanity into God, *theosis*. At the heart of this renewal was F. D. Maurice, and from Maurice there developed a whole movement of thought which emphasized the unity of spirituality and social action and social critique. For Maurice all spirituality was rooted in the social life of the Holy Trinity, and the Kingdom of God was the great underlying reality which was to transform the face of the earth. Not only was spirituality rooted in dogma, but dogma was inseparable from social consciousness. Heather Ward stands firmly in the Maurician tradition as she calls us to a spirituality in which the division of individual and social are removed.

In her exposition of the gift of self, Heather Ward is very close to the theology of Thomas Merton who, in his later writing, was deeply concerned with the question of the true and false self. Merton saw that the dynamic of emptying and of transcendence accurately defines the transformation of our consciousness in Christ. The emptying of the contents of the ego creates a void in which the light of God is manifested. Merton wrote:

Far from establishing one in unassailable narcissistic security, the way of prayer brings us face to face with the sham and indignity of the false self that seeks to live for itself and to enjoy the 'consolations of prayer' for its own sake. This self is pure illusion and ultimately he who lives for and by such an illusion must end either in disgust or madness. *(The Climate of Monastic Prayer,* 1969, pp. 35–6)

I hope that this book will help us all to a deeper understanding of the self and its solidarity in Christ, and will lead us away from self-absorption to an openness to the transforming power of God in Christ.

KENNETH LEECH
London
December 1989

Acknowledgements

An exhaustive list of those to whom I owe thanks would be an exhausting read. Special thanks must go, however, to my husband, Alan, for his encouragement and support, and to our daughter, Frances, for her patience in sharing me with this book; to my niece Coleen Coxon, who typed the manuscript, to Valerie and Brian Coxon, and Margaret Henman, who helped in the preparation of the typescript; and to Canon Leslie Morley who first encouraged me in formulating and writing about these ideas.

The biblical quotations are taken from the Jerusalem Bible, published and copyright 1966, 1967 and 1968 by Darton, Longman and Todd Ltd and Doubleday & Co. Inc., by permission of the publishers.

1

Who am I? – God and myself

'The glory of God is a living man . . .'

There is an old joke about the English traveller deep in the heart of rural Ireland. Hopelessly lost, he chances upon an ancient farmer and asks him for directions to Dublin. 'Ah, to be sure, if it was Dublin I was wanting I shouldn't be starting from here.' A frustrating answer when we are concerned with geography, it is nevertheless a very wise form of response to many of our theological and spiritual questions. All too frequently we begin our exploration from the wrong starting-point, the wrong premise, from which we cannot hope to reach our proper destination. It is, indeed, especially apposite to the issue of selfhood, to the apparent conflicts between self-affirmation and self-denial, 'personal' religion and social involvement which so confuse and disturb many Christians today. This book attempts to offer an alternative starting-point for an exploration into selfhood, a starting-point rooted in the New Testament and the experience of Christians throughout the centuries which enables us to reach a destination at which those dichotomies between affirmation and asceticism, self and society are found to be without foundation. On the journey we will come to an understanding of what it means to say 'I am'.

At present Christians generally offer, it would seem, two mutually exclusive views of selfhood – and all too often within the same sermon, book or conversation! On the one hand 'self' is firmly established as the enemy: 'God first, others second, self last' is fairly representative of the approach. On the other hand we are urged to 'be ourselves' and to envisage

1

the Christian life as a journey towards self-fulfilment. Is the self we must deny the same self we must fulfil or are we trapped by fuzzy terminology? If these 'selves' are different, how and why are they so? These are questions we should, but rarely do, ask. Instead, I suspect, we opt for the view which suits our personality, or swing between the two according to our mood. Today, as Groucho Marx quipped, I would not wish to join any club which would have me for a member, so that 'I crossed out' seems an appropriate approach to my selfhood. Yesterday all things were bright and beautiful, myself included, and I was completely behind a spirituality of self-affirmation. What I need is a coherent vision of the self which puts my yo-yoing subjective experience into a proper theological, spiritual context, which enables me to understand the muddle that is me in the light of God's creating and saving activity. Our present approaches to selfhood cannot do this because each begins from inadequate or incomplete premises.

The vision behind the slogan 'God first, others second, self last' does justice neither to God nor to his creatures. God is here seen as *a* being, to be ranked with other beings; greater, more powerful, but still an individual entity who stands over against lesser, weaker entities. 'Others' take on, through their ranking, a greater value as entities over against self at the bottom of the heap. It suggests no relationship between God who was foolish enough to create my distinct self and the 'others' he created than that of inferiority. Both God and humankind are reduced. God is no longer 'I AM', the one 'in whom we live and move and have our being' (Acts 17:28). My brothers and sisters are perceived to have no bonds of mutuality with me, no common destiny. Nowhere, in this approach, is it stressed that I am equally an 'other' to the self of parents, siblings, friends, colleagues, husband, children, and thus equally owed respect and concern. This may read as wilful misrepresentation of a slogan more often repeated than pondered, but experience of depressive illness, my own and that of others, confirms my belief that this is the general effect of this kind of presentation of 'self'.

Gradually our use of this word 'self' has become identified only with such terms as 'selfish', 'self-seeking', 'self-regard',

2

so that 'self' denotes only what is evil or negative. It was something of a shock to me, despite previous awareness of the prevailing attitude, to be informed on one occasion that my research into the vision of selfhood in literature was an improper subject for a Christian!

Such a loss of the concept of the self has enabled us to use it, negatively, as a powerful means of control, both in personal relationships and in social life. How easy it is for the parent or the government official, possessors of power, to label as 'selfish', as a denial of their rights as 'others', any action of the less powerful which refuses to meet their every demand, however illegitimate. How many people have been damaged by the insistence that any aspiration, any desire, any need not sanctioned by its meeting of another's aspiration, desire or need is necessarily rank selfishness, and have therefore never learned to handle these positively? I think of the elderly lady, Monica, sunk in the deepest depression, who considers every personal wish to be sinful; of the Roman Catholic priest in his forties who took to the bottle and to outlandish garb and behaviour when suddenly overwhelmed by desires and needs which had become chaotic and unmanageable because hitherto unacknowledged. I think of my friend, Helen, with anorexia nervosa, who can only express her rightful needs through the state of her body, while simultaneously revealing, physically, the power of the idea that 'I crossed out' is the only acceptable attitude to the self. These, perhaps, are at the extremes, but they illustrate the way in which our understanding of the self in a purely negative way has seeped into our culture and informed it with a sub-Christian vision of the human person.

It is hardly surprising, then, that against such a view has arisen the contrary emphasis on the 'goodness' of the self and the consequent loss of the separate term to such expressions as 'self-fulfilment', 'self-affirmation'. No longer is the Christian life a journey to God but a 'journey to self-discovery'. Our pilgrimage in life is now a quest for self-fulfilment. In these contexts 'self' is used synonymously with 'personality': spiritual growth, in this approach, means the expansion of our personality, the removal of blockages in our emotional and imaginative life, and therefore in our social relationships.

With this 'self-fulfilment' as our goal spiritual life is essentially well-functioning psychological life, as we find in Gerard Hughes's *God of Surprises*:

> Our treasure lies in our inner life . . . In religious language this inner life is called 'the soul', and the art of knowing it, healing it and harmonizing its forces is called spirituality. Religion should encourage us to become more aware of this inner life and should teach us how to befriend it, for it is the source of our strength and storehouse of our wisdom.

Once again the vision of God and of man is reduced. No longer is Christ our strength and wisdom: man has his separate storehouse. God is the servant of our 'personal development' while man loses his nature as a *spiritual* being, whose capacity for response to God is not dependent on the structure of individual personalities.

Such an equation of the spiritual with the psychological not only denies the validity of the biblical picture of manhood as defined by the reception of God's Spirit (Genesis 2:7), it also opens the door to the reduction of human beings to their biological functions. Once personality, the result of our psychological make-up, is regarded as the key to selfhood, the source of personal worth, how do we answer the brain scientist's contention that mind or personality is no more than an epiphenomenon, a side-product, of brain function? Or the social anthropologist's belief that 'human nature' is a fallacious concept, personality being infinitely malleable by cultures? Alter the chemical balance in my brain and my personality alters; I become extroverted and full of imaginative ideas or depressed and morbidly receptive to any hint of my guiltiness or uselessness. Am I then more or less of a person than I was previously? Does my worth as a human being depend upon achieving physiological equilibrium? And if my culture fosters a personality cold, indifferent to human suffering and regarding loving as weakness, does this make me impermeable to the gospel? That is, is God bound by the human structure which produces our personalities, so that the process of conversion necessitates a complete re-creation of our personality in its totality? Our answer to this must be no, for any study of famous 'converts' such as St Paul and St

Augustine, and any review of our own experience of conversion, testifies to a combination of continuity and a radical
reorientation.

Both of our current approaches to selfhood seem to lead us
to very different, but equally undesirable, destinations. The
former leads to a life-denying 'Crosstianity', which negates
the goodness and wisdom of God in creating free and unique
human persons. The second leads us to a humanism in Christian garb, in which the pursuit of a 'good' self subtly displaces
the quest for a transcendent God. Borne within this vision
are the seeds of its own destruction. Can we identify a third
starting-point then, a starting-point which will lead us to our
desired destination of understanding our selfhood in relationship to God? Have we access to a vision of the self which
does justice to our apprehension of the glory of God made
known in his creatures while simultaneously acknowledging
the experience of wretchedness and alienation which is theirs?

I am convinced that such a vision is available to us through
taking seriously both St Paul's concept of the person, as, not
body and soul, but body, soul and *spirit* and its development
by such Fathers of the early Church as Irenaeus of Lyons.
Irenaeus' understanding of selfhood is no dry-as-dust theory
but a way of entry into the richness of St Paul's understanding
of man renewed in Christ and an invitation to experience all
life as gift, an invitation offered to me experientially at the
turning-point of depressive illness.

During my sickness I had come to believe that I had
committed 'the unforgivable sin', that I could not be saved
because I lacked an 'ingredient' essential for being human.
The power of the delusion or fantasy was very strong, but I
was sufficiently free, at intervals, to recognize it as a magnifi-
cation of my 'normal' conviction that I had to earn salvation
by virtue of my personality, by virtue of the qualities I possessed as a person. I had to be able to justify my existence
in terms of talents, abilities and capacity for love and sponta-
neity before God would have anything to do with me. Gradually I came to feel that I must surrender the fantasy, that I
must express to God a faith that he was greater than my
conviction of damnation: a faith in the possibility of the
impossible. I spent an evening saying simply 'Yes', yes to

whatever was the truth about God and about myself. In the back of my mind reverberated long-forgotten words from a poem by Gerard Manley Hopkins, words which run like a golden thread through my life and through the writing of this book:

> I am all at once what Christ is, since he
>   was what I am, and
> This Jack, joke, poor potsherd, patch,
>   matchwood, immortal diamond,
> Is immortal diamond.

There came no sudden revelation, no lightning flash of inspiration, but quietly for some days after this I was aware of what I can only call light: a warm, powerful, loving light outside me, and a small, answering light within, an energy which I knew came from the light beyond and yet was me, was my *life*, my worth, while yet being nothing to do with my attributes, with anything I had called 'me' or mine. This light, this energy, was pure gift and was both 'me' and not me. It was the core of my existence yet it brought no sense of possession, of belonging to me by right; it was a gift of light from light. There was no question of my being *of myself* part of that greater light, as though I was just one separated particle; that, too, would have resulted in an appropriation of the light to myself. I only knew that I was 'I' in so far as I received this light. So I, who had previously wanted to hide my 'ugly' (that is, non-human) face from others was no longer afraid to be seen, for it was no longer my features which would be seen, I felt, but the light within.

One powerful fantasy replacing another? Perhaps; but if so, then God was using such fantasy to teach truth. The most important effect of this experience was the sense of urgency it left behind about the need to live with my light turned towards 'The Light'. Rather than producing any sense of wealth in myself it made me aware of the need to be turned outwards to 'The Light', keeping above all in constant orientation to it, and of the inadequacy and poverty of what I had called 'myself' before the greatness of the gift. I was like a child who had asked for a bird's egg, expecting that of a wren, and had been given an ostrich nest. Awareness of the glory that God calls us to share was coupled then with consciousness of the need for repentance and of the truth of humility.

The second major consequence was an awakened capacity to celebrate the existence of other people and of the natural world. Rather than supplanting the material with the spiritual, this knowledge of life as gift produced great joy in the sheer being of whatever surrounded me. There was tenderness for people and for creation, everything took on a substantiality it had hitherto lacked and at times seemed suffused with light. 'The heavens are telling the glory of God' no longer seemed poetic licence.

At this point I was alerted to the theology of light within the Orthodox Church, and found in the Fathers of the undivided Church such as St Irenaeus a vision of manhood which not only made sense of the experiences both of depression and of light, but also answered so many of my questions about the meaning of selfhood.

Many people, if they have heard of St Irenaeus at all, know only that he was responsible for that currently popular dictum 'The glory of God is a living man' (or 'Man fully alive'). Heard within our modern frame of reference this seems in perfect accord with our popular spirituality of affirmation. Like all slogans, however, this is open to misinterpretation through quotation out of context, and, in this instance, in two important ways.

Irenaeus' affirmation of the value of man is but half of the story, for he continues, 'but the glory of man is the vision of God'. Far from emphasizing the value of man's experience for its own sake Irenaeus is stressing the fact that the fullness of humanity is only attained when man is totally with God. God, not man, must be the measure of human fulfilment.

More important still for our understanding of the self is Irenaeus' approach to the very notion of 'manhood'. Today the phrase 'a living man' would suggest to most people an individual, separate personality with particular attributes distinguishing that personality from others. We no longer tend to consider the idea of 'man' except as an abstract concept. It has not always been so. For the Fathers of the Church it was possible to speak of 'man' in a way which denoted, not an abstract generalization like 'humanity', but the state of each human being, whose particularity yet expresses the complete nature of humankind. Theologians such as Irenaeus based this thinking about human selfhood on the account of Creation in Genesis and on the Pauline account of man as body-soul-spirit.

For these thinkers the opening chapters of Genesis are central: man is made in the image of God, made to reflect God. To retain that likeness to God the image must remain in relationship with the source. Man has dignity by virtue of his Creator, but has no independent identity as a *man* apart from him. Furthermore we see that in Genesis 2 what makes 'a living man' is the breath of God: only when the creature who is made from the dust of the earth, like other creatures, has also the gift of God's breath, his Spirit, is he truly able to live as a person.

Man's disobedience of God, therefore, damages him because the image is, through it, wrenched away from the source. Man made to reflect God's glory chooses to 'go it alone'. Christ's obedience as man, and his assumption of our estrangement from God, reconciles the image and the source once more, making possible the fulfilment of the image of God within us.

Such is the framework within which Irenaeus understands the Pauline division of the person into spirit-soul-body. Man living as a body-soul entity, as only an embodied personality, our modern 'individual', is not yet fully a human person:

> There are three elements of which . . . the complete man is made up, flesh, soul and spirit: one of these preserves and fashions the man, and this is spirit; another is given unity and form by the first, and this is flesh; the third, the soul, is mid-way between the two and sometimes it is subservient to the spirit and is raised by it; while sometimes it allies itself with flesh and descends to earthly passions . . . When this spirit is mingled with soul and united with created matter then through the outpouring of the Spirit, the complete man is produced: this is man in the image of God. A man with soul only, lacking spirit, is 'psychic': such a man is carnal, unfinished, incomplete.

To become a self is therefore to bring to full expression our spiritual nature, opening it up to God and bringing the psycho-physical aspects of our being into harmony with him. The core of our selfhood may be seen, therefore, as the spiritual nature, restored to us in Christ, rather than the physical, mental and emotional attributes which derive from the nature we share with other animals, that is, from our inheritance as creatures of the earth.

It becomes possible therefore to speak of the fully actualized self as a perfected human image of God, who reflects the whole being of Man within his or her particularized identity, as the Persons of the Trinity encompass the fullness of Godhood within their distinctiveness.

We must not, however, reify selfhood, considering it as a bundle of qualities, as it were. St Irenaeus thinks of the self as basically a capacity for receiving and responding to God, not as a pre-existing entity. It is 'through the outpouring of Spirit' being received by the human spirit that the 'complete' person is made. The essence of our selfhood resides in our capacity for continuing acceptance of the gift of God's life-giving Spirit: the receptiveness of our spirit to the Holy Spirit then allows the activation of the gifts we have from God by nature; that is, our specific psychological and physical attributes.

Selfhood, then, is the capacity for God which is our existence itself, which informs and directs our personality. Consequently, just as we can say 'I am *through* my body', without equating our selfhood with our ever-changing physical substance, so we can also say 'I am *through* my personality' without equating our identity with a mental and emotional life equally susceptible to change and decay.

As we have seen it so far, the personality, Irenaeus' 'psyche', is morally neutral, and becomes the means of good when it is directed Godwards by our spirit. The problem begins for Man when psyche allies with 'flesh', that is, when the personality apprehends only its physical and material aspects, its embodiedness, and takes this as the sum total of its identity. Doing thus amounts to a unilateral declaration of independence, for the personality can look to its own qualities as its inviolable possessions, possessions which deny any need to recognize derivation and which seem to distinguish it from all others. So when 'psyche' allies with 'flesh', we have the breeding-ground for rebellion against God. 'Carnal' man chooses to become 'like God' by his own action, to become godlike in himself, rather than to receive this state as a gift. This is the sin of Adam, to deny dependence and derivation. In Genesis Adam's sin is followed by that of Cain: of denying relationship with another. Once Man has chosen personality as his centre the sense of being the recipient of the gift of life disappears: 'carnal man' is the 'self-made man' – autonomous, isolated, self-sufficient, and 'king of his own castle'.

If 'self' denotes our sense of full identity we can see that, accurately used, it is the appropriate term for Irenaeus' 'spiritual' man. We may therefore use self exclusively for the active receptivity within us which turns outwards to God, in acceptance of life as a gift. It is this 'selfhood' which Christians are called upon to affirm and fulfil.

Irenaeus' 'carnal' man, which includes our psychological self-image, self-definition and self-awareness, we may call 'ego'. It is this 'ego', with its tendency to turn man inwards upon himself as the source and sustainer of his being, which is the 'self' of such terms as 'selfishness'. The call to self-denial is, in truth, the call to 'ego-denial', in which denial means not negation of existence but denial of claims and pretensions. To deny ego is to refuse it the centrality and autonomy to which it tends.

The spiritual 'self', therefore, has not refused recognition of the attributes and wounds of its ego; it acknowledges being through them but also stands free from them, knowing that ego is neither source nor identity. Ego is subordinated to the claims of spirit and, thus integrated with it, is directed Godwards. However, our normal experience is of conflict between our spirit's openness-to-God and our ego's introversion. In discussion, therefore, terms need to be used with some flexibility. 'Self' must frequently be used to denote spiritual identity as it stands over against the pretensions to independence of the ego. Similarly ego, used in opposition to self, will denote the personality when it is held as the source, sustainer and purpose of its own existence.

From this starting-point of the self as God's image in Man

and the distinction between selfhood and ego, we may begin to see our desired destination. We may discern a developing picture of Man which affirms the goodness and glory for which he is created while accepting his alienation and fallenness. Affirmation and denial, fulfilment and sacrifice begin to be seen as complementary rather than conflicting demands. We may begin to glimpse, too, a vision of selfhood which transcends opposition between individual and society, individual and creation. Each person belongs to God and to the earth, while sharing with every other human being the same image of God, the same gift of openness to God.

We find, too, in this vision of the self a new awakening to the truths of those gospel paradoxes that we must, indeed, die in order to live, lose in order to gain, become poor as the only way to be rich. It enables us to welcome with joy the contradiction that the self can only be all that it is made to be when it sees itself as being and having nothing, when it is content to be a simple capacity for God. Through it we come to perceive that only when unimpeded by ego can God fully energize us with his life so that we can truly say, 'I live and yet not I, but Christ living in me'.

The divided self

'My me is God . . .'

I remember the shock and the excitement with which, as a
teenager, I greeted the information that atoms and the solid
artefacts of our material world must be understood as bundles
of energy and not 'things', 'objects'. Shock, because it seemed
to contradict commonsense experience, excitement because
the world suddenly seemed alive and active, with a potential,
a power of which I had hitherto been unaware. I suspect that
there is a similar initial difficulty in accepting a view of the
self as 'a capacity for God'. Often when trying to talk about
such an idea of the self we necessarily use images suggestive
of 'thing-ness'. 'Capacity' can tend to give the impression of
the self as an empty vessel waiting to be filled, while the idea
of the 'empty space' again implies the existence of some thing
which has withdrawn. Such images are frequently useful and
necessary (and I shall, indeed, employ them). It is vital,
however, that we see them for what they are, images, ways
of talking about what is dynamic.

Behind our images of entities must be an idea of potential,
of energy. The self is a capacity for God in much the same
way as a metal has a capacity to conduct electricity, to receive
and transmit an energy from beyond itself. And like a metal,
in appropriate conditions, it may become 'superconductive',
offering no resistance to the energy it receives. If we say,
therefore, that the self must grow, it is easy to see that by
growth is meant, not increase in size or in the number or
quality of attributes, but increased responsiveness to God,
increased receptiveness to his Spirit. We have also seen that

ego is often the enemy to such development of our potential. For the self to become what it is made to be, to realize its fullness as a capacity for God, there must be a growing freedom from the ego and a thoroughgoing reorientation towards God, a process equivalent to the superconductivity produced in metal by altering the conditions in which it is kept and thereby minimizing resistance.

It follows, therefore, that in order to reach my self, my capacity for God, there must be a deep, often painful, lifelong experience of dying to ego. Since man in his state of estrangement from God regards his ego as *himself*, the experience of ego-denial, of removing the desires, needs and illusions of the ego from centre stage is perceived as an act of undoing, of disintegration, of loss of all that we have called ourselves and our lives. What, from the point of view of our ego is destructive is, from that of our self, supremely constructive: we are through it brought increasingly into the life of God, with our powers of mind and body liberated from the demands of sustaining the vision of self-sufficient ego.

Understood in this way, becoming oneself is another way of talking about repentance. We are accustomed to thinking of repentance as 'turning round to face in the other direction'. I would suggest that it is helpful to take this a stage further and envisage it as 'turning oneself inside-out, to face in the opposite direction'. Ego makes of us a closed system around the needs, flaws and attributes with which we set about to win or deserve our existence, acceptance and salvation. Denying to ego that centrality means that we must truly empty ourselves out by turning outwards to the God who gives us life and spirit whereby to receive his Spirit. We must cease living as possessors and discover ourselves as beings made to receive our existence and identity from beyond ourselves. This process of repentance, ego-denial, entails the acceptance of complete spiritual poverty and the development of humility based upon acknowledgement of derivation from earth and dependence upon God.

To many ears this insistence on humility and poverty grates: it smacks of grovelling before God and of a refusal to accept human maturity and worth. Too often we have, indeed, had urged upon us a humility which falsifies reality;

13

how many of us remember those injunctions against boasting which led us to never admitting our capacity for any kind of achievement or understanding? How often have we been seduced into using 'humility' as an excuse for not taking risks, for doing less than we are able? How often have our neurotic fears been labelled 'humility' and therefore never acknowledged?

I well recall that my own deep-seated fear of academic failure and lack of creativity was designated 'scholarly humility' (at age seventeen!) leaving me to equate this with a paralysing lack of self-confidence. I suspect it has been so for many of us, because our confusion between self and ego has led us to understand humility wrongly as primarily an attitude towards our personality attributes. If we consider it closely we shall see that this is misguided.

Humility is concerned with 'knowing of what we are made', knowing that we owe our life and gifts wholly to the gratuitous love of God but also that we come from humus, the earth, and share its frailty. Humility, as St Francis de Sales never tired of saying, establishes us in the truth about ourselves, the truth about our utter reliance on God, which prevents our holding our personality as our centre. It therefore brings true *confidence* and *freedom* with regard to that personality, in two ways. First, since my personal gifts are not 'me' but gifts, they are purely for my use, needing neither justification nor concealment. They are not statements about my human worth. Secondly, this humility grounds me in confidence in God: when I know my life is in his hands, not mine, I am free to risk my personality, to launch into unknown territory (like writing this book) because neither my failure and inadequacy nor any measure of success can fundamentally alter that truth. The only fear left to me is that of turning away, of trying to take myself out of his hands.

In my own life I have painfully come to see this principle operating: after years of crippling diffidence I will now accept, with some natural misgivings, offers from which I would earlier have shrunk or run away (as I did, quite literally, from my first university), because I no longer need to earn the right to existence through possessing a 'good', 'useful' or 'successful' personality. Despite constant failure in practice,

I know that I am free to let God and others be my concern
while I am his. Humility is the basis for all our ego-denial
and is therefore gloriously positive. As St Francis de Sales,
that wise guide, has said, there is but one pair of wings for
our journey to God, each wing essential to the other – distrust
in our ego and trust in God.

Humility frees us in one other crucial way, for it liberates
our proclamation of *the gift* – of the eternal, transfigured life
made available to us through the incarnation, death and
resurrection of Jesus. Humility allows us to revel in the truth
that we are 'bound for glory' because we know that the gift
is entirely gratuitous, saying nothing at all about us and our
'deserts' and everything about the goodness of God. In this
sense humility is the root of joy, as I believe that great
Anglican theologian, F. D. Maurice discovered. Maurice was,
as it were, intoxicated by the thought of Man's sonship to
God in and through the sonship of Christ. He was also keenly
aware of Man's fallenness and incapacity apart from God.
Maurice knew that these two apprehensions belong together,
that humility is the way to largeness of spirit, as he reveals
in a letter to a friend:

> Hope – hope that I, the meanest of God's creatures, for
> such to myself I must appear, am destined for the noblest
> purposes and the highest glory – is that which alone can
> make me humble and keep me so . . .
> . . . you must aspire high if you would know yourself
> nothing. If you would feel yourself to be the worm that you
> are you must claim your privilege of being like God.

Maurice points us towards that other problematic word,
'nothing'. Today, saying 'I am nothing' may more often than
not be regarded as symptomatic of neurosis, and so it may
be. It is, however, as we have seen, in one important sense,
the truth. When the Lord said to St Catherine of Siena, 'You
are she that is not', he was not denying that she existed but
he was refusing her the right to say 'I am' at the same level
at which he can say 'I am'. Only God, I AM, may say 'I'
without reference to another; as George MacDonald puts it:

Thou art the only person and I cry

Unto the father of this my 'I'.

To acknowledge being nothing is to acknowledge that our
selfhood comes from God. It may also mean accepting being
no-thing; accepting that our 'I' cannot be circumscribed by
our self-image and ego-awareness, and so affirming that we
are created to reflect and share the Allness, the No-thingness,
of God. Hence total poverty ushers us into the realm of God.
It is in this light that we must read the asceticism of all our
spiritual guides when they insist upon the nothingness of the
self or the self's identity with God. When, for example, St
John of the Cross counsels:

> To arrive at possessing all, desire to possess nothing,
> To arrive at being all, desire to be nothing,

he is urging the same dispossession from ego, not from self,
that is found in positive terms in the teaching of St Catherine
of Genoa: 'My me is God, nor do I recognize any other me
except my God himself.' For both these lovers of God, one a
contemplative friar, the other a married woman of immense
activity, knowing the nothingness of the ego is the way into
the plenitude awaiting the self who is freed to love and enjoy
the world as God loves and enjoys it:

> Mine are the heavens and mine is the earth. Mine are the
> nations, the just are mine and mine are the sinners. The
> angels are mine and Mother of God and all things are
> mine: and God himself is mine and for me because Christ
> is mine and all for me. What do you ask then and seek,
> my soul? Yours is all this and all this is for you. Do not
> engage in something less, nor pay heed to the crumbs which
> fall from your Father's table. Go forth and exult in your
> glory!

For St John of the Cross and all who urge this radical dispossession of ego, true self-denial lies in clinging to ego, eating
the 'crumbs from the table': it leads to spiritual inanition and
death. By contrast, the 'death' involved in the dethronement
from the centre of our ego leads to fullness of life in God.
This is the core of the gospel teaching that the one who loses
his life for God's sake will find it. We are all called to some

kind of 'martyrdom', being prepared to surrender all that we have in order to remain open to God: life is to be lived as a returnable gift and not as a possession to be defended at all costs.

Although repentance is achieved through 'surrender', through 'abandonment' to God of our concern with ego, such terms do not imply lack of effort and responsibility on our part, nor does the concept of self as gift suggest bland passivity as our model of being. There is required of us an active co-operation with, a willing responsiveness to, the actions of God and a readiness to exercise choice. Before each of us lies the option discerned by George MacDonald:

> Shall I be born of God, or of mere man?
> Be made like Christ, or on some other plan?

We can choose to respond to the gift of spirit or to ignore it, in concentration upon ego. To become what it is made to be the spirit must co-operate, work with, the Spirit. We must become, as it were, 'parents' to ourselves, nurturing to fulfilment by our choices the self which is being made by God. God does not force himself on us but leaves us free to be responsible for the use we make of his gift.

This necessity of choice emphasizes the place of the will in the actualization of the self and leads us to making a distinction when we speak of the will parallel to that between self and ego. We need, in fact, to think in terms of two wills in Man. In his spirit Man has, by virtue of his creation as an image of God, a 'will-to-God' or 'will-to-good'; in his ego, his psycho-physical being, he has a natural will to self-preservation which he shares with the rest of nature, linking him with the cycle of procreation, life and decay. For our self to become itself the will-to-God must be constantly exercised. George MacDonald, again, discerns this need of the created will to unite its energy with the will of the Creator, if the self is to know its destiny of participation in the life of God:

> The life that hath not willed itself to be
> Must clasp the life that willed and be at peace
> Or, like a leaf, wind-blown, through chaos flee;
> A life husk into which the demons go . . .

But when I turn and grasp the making hand
And will the making will, with confidence
I ride the crest of the creation-wave,
Helpless no more, no more existence's slave;
In the heart of love's creating fire I stand,
And, love-possessed in heart and soul and sense,
Take up the making share the making Master gave.

This is by no means an easy concept to grasp, for we are accustomed to considering the will as an attribute of personality, with moral overtones (as when we speak of willpower). If we take note only of the natural will then those whose genetic endowment and social background produce weak-willed personalities would seem predetermined for failure in making the moral choices required for self-realization. The concept of the spiritual will-to-God liberates us from this vision of determinacy and gives us confidence in our capacity to transcend the confines of ego. We are free to exercise our will for salvation and life in God and, indeed, must be in the constant process of exercising it. Just as God's continuing act of will sustains our existence so must our will be continually engaged in sustaining directedness towards him.

It would seem impossible to talk about selfhood without encountering paradoxes both in concept and language. This particular paradox of active willing and receptivity, with its attendant notions of surrender and passivity, may be a particularly difficult one for us to grasp. I have found it helpfully conveyed in the images of gestation and birth. I have already mentioned the idea of our being 'parents' to ourselves, nurturing what is ours and yet not ours, just as the child comes of its parents and yet does not belong to them. Parenting may help us understand our activity, gestation our responsive passivity. If the self is the image of God in us, then it is quite possible to think of that self as a 'Christ-self', an image of the perfect image, into which God is shaping us with our co-operation. We can thus think of the process of self-actualization as the gestation of Christ within us, of a life developing in us which is both of us and yet not ours. Like the pregnant mother we must protect our state of 'primary maternal pre-occupation', focusing our concern and our energy upon what

18

nourishes the development of the 'child' within, rather than on our ego. In this way we must be active and vigilant, guarding against those powers within and beyond ourselves which would damage or abort the inner life. Yet, like the mother-to-be we must also 'let it be', allowing the child to take what it will of us and be formed according to its own logic. The mother cannot *make* the child: while providing material for its formation she cannot claim it as her creation. It is here that we feel the full force of the gospel saying that we cannot add to our own stature. We must be content with a secret life growing according to principles of which we are only dimly aware.

This idea of 'inner motherhood' is one of those convictions which arose slowly out of reflection upon psychological experience: the psyche may, indeed, provide material for the Spirit. Some years ago I spent a week in silence at Taizé, praying daily before the community's icon of Mary and her Child, without any conscious reflections on the subject. I went home feeling psychologically very strong and later could only ascribe this to the realization that, psychologically speaking, I could mother my own inner hurt child quite well, that I could be both strong and vulnerable. It seemed that the icon had triggered a mental response, possibly crystallizing ideas already gathered elsewhere.

Much later it became clear that, as I was approaching it, the making ready of a space within for the Lord, my normal approach to prayer, was in fact, a very maternal activity. I had regularly used as a kind of mantra an old antiphon, 'Come, Lord, and visit us in peace, that we may rejoice before you with a perfect heart', and now became acutely aware of the 'heart', the inner sanctuary of the self, as a womb, as it were, in which Christ was to be nurtured: we were all, I felt, asked to offer the 'humble space' to be made fruitful by the overshadowing of the Spirit. Such an approach seemed to do justice to the necessity both of taking responsibility for our selfhood in creating the most favourable conditions and of passivity, in eschewing any attempt to predetermine and shape ourselves. Later still I discovered, with some surprise, that this had been a not uncommon image for the growth of the self, an image whose disappearance accompanied the loss of our concept of spiritual selfhood. The most beautiful expression of this is found in a sermon by Guerric of Igny, an insufficiently well-known Cistercian abbot of the twelfth century:

Behold the unspeakable condescension of God and at the same time the power of the mystery which passes all understanding. He who created you is created in you, and as if it were too little that you should possess the father, he wishes also that you would become a mother to himself. 'Whoever', he says, 'does the will of my father is my brother and sister and mother.' O faithful soul, open wide your bosom, expand your affections, admit no constraint in your heart, conceive him whom creation cannot contain. Open to the Word of God an ear that will listen. This is the way to the womb of the heart for the Spirit who brings about conception; in such fashion are the bones of Christ, that is the virtues, built up in the pregnant womb.

Thanks be to you, Spirit, who breathe where you will. By your gift I see not one but countless faithful souls pregnant with that noble offspring. Preserve your works, lest anyone should suffer miscarriage and expel, shapeless and dead, the progeny he has conceived of God.

Taking gestation as an image for self-actualization also helps our understanding of two other aspects of that process: its hiddenness and its incompleteness. We cannot *see* the baby growing in the womb, we can only exercise faith and hope; we know the child, and yet the relationship is not complete because the knowledge is incomplete. We must wait in expectant patience. And once the child is delivered these elements of hiddenness and incompleteness remain: the baby's identity will only slowly unfold and always will retain some mystery to itself. So it is with our selfhood.

Our thinking may be further helped if we allow the image of the foetus to be transformed into that of the seed, as used of the Kingdom in the Gospels. What Jesus says of the Kingdom-as-seed may be paralleled with the Kingdom within, the kingly reign of God in our selfhood. The seed of the Kingdom, we are told, is one which grows in secret, we know not how; it is unavailable to our scrutiny and measure-

20

ment. And the fruit of this seed is in some way already among us, while its full realization lies in the future. The 'eschatological tension' of the already and the not yet, which we experience on the large scale, as a people of God, as the waiting and groaning for the liberation of our bodies (Romans 8:19–23) is also the truth for each person: our selfhood is present to us, as our capacity for God, but it is not yet fully actualized; to return to the earlier image of the metal, it is not yet super-conductive. Our identity will not be known to us until we are fully and finally 'in Christ', and the process of detachment from ego has been completed. Baptized into the death and resurrection of Christ, our selves, which are to be channels for his life in the world, are hidden from us, with Christ in God, as St Paul assures us (Colossians 3:3).

If we understand our selves as a capacity for God and that it is this capacity, given us by virtue of our creation in God's image, which is the core of our ability to say 'I', it follows that, unlike the ego, it is not open to our observation and analysis.

Becoming our selves thus demands willingness to forgo the need for rational, distinct knowledge of our true and final identity. Our hope regarding this must be placed in the God who is its source and its end, as 1 John 3:2–3 teaches:

> It does not yet appear what we shall be, but we know that when he appears we shall be like him, for we shall see him as he is. And everyone who thus hopes in him purifies himself as he is pure.

We are to 'look to him and be radiant' (Psalm 33:6). As I learned with such immediacy in the experience of Light, we are not to concentrate on knowing the lineaments of our own face but on looking towards the One who transforms us into himself, making us reflections of his glory, as St Paul understood in his consideration of Moses' meeting with God:

> And we with our unveiled faces reflecting like mirrors the brightness of the Lord, all grow brighter and brighter as we are turned into the image that we reflect: this is the work of the Lord who is Spirit. (2 Corinthians 3:18)

Such an acceptance of hiddenness brings freedom from

21

concern with our own roots and spiritual temperature (cf. 2 Corinthians 3:17). It locates our hope in God; it assures us that, however amorphous or diminished we feel our egos to be, if we are continually repenting, then the basic development of our selfhood is secure: we are being made to conform to Christ, to express God's way of being human. In our struggle of repentance we may keep the external figure of Christ before us, as teacher and model of the way of loving sacrifice, but we should do so in the knowledge that this outward, conscious imitation of Christ is not refashioning us against the grain. Rather, as St John suggests, the purification that we undergo will ultimately reveal to us a selfhood already modelled on his: we will have developed according to the proper logic of our creation. This is all we need to know of our identity.

If I only finally discover my full identity in seeing God, it follows that the human experience of being such a self must be one of incompleteness: we can know only the process, the way, and not the destination. Whereas the ego may set for itself defined limits and defined goals, the self is called to share in the boundlessness of God. God is continually making us into the image of himself, the infinite One. Thus all our experiences of changeableness and diminution are means of keeping us from the fantasy of completeness, and bringing us into fuller awareness of our participation now in eternal life, infinite life. This aspect of our selfhood is clarified for us by St Gregory of Nyssa:

> The sovereign and highest Good, whose nature is goodness, is the divine nature itself. Now – since the only limitation of virtue is vice, and since the divine nature excludes anything that is contrary to it, then it follows that the divine nature is conceived without bound or limit. But the soul that pursues true virtue actually participates in God Himself because He is infinite virtue. Now since those who have come to know the highest good desire to share completely in it and since this good is limitless, it follows that their desire must necessarily be co-extensive with the limitless and therefore have no limit. Thus it is absolutely impossible to attain perfection . . . How can a man reach the boundary

he is looking for if it does not exist? . . . perfection lies in never stopping in our growth in good.

The extension of the self, like that of the Kingdom, knows no bounds when it is in God. In our present state ego at once inflates our vision of our natural capacities and diminishes our hope of glory. For the self to enter that glory the illusions and pretences of ego must be deflated. The question remains for us, 'how'?

3

Becoming myself – a way of life

'Holiness before peace'

The call to 'empty yourself' may come as something very daunting and very mysterious. As an overly self-conscious adolescent I agonized over this phrase, recognizing in it something that I wanted and yet unable to see either what it meant or how to go about it. It has taken a long time for any light to dawn and for me to come to realize that emptying myself does not mean pretending that I do not exist and living in apology for my temerity in so doing, nor does it mean becoming vapid, with no opinions, ideas and aspirations, the empty house into which more demons may rush. Rather, it means setting God and the truths of my existence in him at the centre of my being and acting, holding my feelings, needs, aspirations and so on at arm's length, as it were, so that they do not constitute my truth and my being. Having grasped this, the 'how' seems easier to discern, and the traditional 'disciplines' of spiritual life – prayer, recollection, reading, fasting, vigil – take on a fuller significance.

A common tendency is to regard these disciplines as a means of getting us into shape, training us as 'spiritual athletes' who can exercise a firm will and self-control. Fasting, especially, may be seen as a means of acquiring spiritual power. Alternatively, fasting and vigil have often been understood punitively, as a means of correcting and chastising wayward senses. The links with our two rejected views of the self are quite clear. I suggest that we should consider all our spiritual practices as ways of helping us to starve the ego of its needs, by refusing it the attention and the centrality it demands and by developing within us an habitual attentiveness to the reality of God.

So much is written today about prayer that what follows is offered with some trepidation. My purpose is not a detailed discussion but a highlighting of principles. If it is distressingly familiar to you, I would suggest you move on to the next topic.

Prayer, as I understand it, is primarily something which God does in me, it is allowing God to flow through me. My part is to make myself available for this, to become consciously with, and in, the God who is always with, and in, me. Consequently, however much I may feel to be the initiator I am, in fact, always responding to a pressure, a hint, an invitation from him. Our ego may desire us to be on equal terms with the Lord, determining the time and place for the meeting, but it is not so. The dethronement of ego begins with this recognition and continues when we grasp its corollary that prayer is to make us available to God and not the other way round. Prayer easily becomes need-centred, consolation-centred, experience-centred: we pray for what God does for *us*, for the strength he gives *us*, for the satisfaction of feeling with him. All too often we feel that our prayer is totally for God because we have brought all our troubles to him, acknowledging our need, but then praying from within our distress becomes immersion in it. We do not leave our problems with him but continue to chase them round in his presence. Gradually attention has been diverted from God in himself towards our ego, with God as its helper.

Awareness of this tendency leads me to centre all prayer, therefore, in adoration, understood not as one aspect of prayer but as its underpinning and context. Adoration seems to be a word little used and little understood. When I was teaching on an Anglican Readers' course, any response to the subject of adoration was always a comment on praise! The two terms were considered interchangeable expressions of gladness and thankfulness to God for his attributes and actions. That is my understanding of praise: it tends towards God for *what* he is, and generally, what he is to, and for, us. Adoration is sheer wonder *that* he is, and desires simply to let him be. It is an attitude of awe, mixed with longing and with love, in

25

the apprehension of God as loving holiness. It is not the dread-ful awe of the idol-worshipper before the fretful and naked power of his deity but the knowledge of the presence of a Goodness which draws us to itself. The response to this is self-forgetfulness, reduction to insignificance, accompanied by the total inadequacy of our powers of expression, which leads us to silence and prostration, in spirit if not in body. This prostration in spirit is no grovelling but a joyful revelling in the Allness of God. He *is*; nothing else matters because all that is of worth is in him. Adoration therefore confirms us in the truth of humility and poverty, opening us to participation in the God who is all, freeing us to delight wholly in him.

It follows that adoration, with its attendant spiritual poverty, may inform all our prayer. Praise for what God is and does springs out of such adoration and ensures that the focus remains Godward, that attention remains directed towards the Giver and not to the happiness and fortune of the beneficiaries.

Similarly, adoration may inform our prayer of confession, driving out concern with ego. It ensures that the recognition of our failure to respond to God's loving holiness does not become an egocentric wallowing in shame. Attention in confession needs to be firmly fixed on the God whose love has been rejected or lightly treated, rather than on our own awfulness which so frequently transfixes us like the gaze of the Gorgon.

Awareness of God's transcendence keeps us little, prevents the ego from inflating itself by claims to greatness in sin, if robbed elsewhere. The spirit of adoration helps us to confront with serenity the greatest need – to admit, not our depths, which may satisfy our taste for grandeur, but our shallows, our essential tendency to triviality, to security, to comfort: 'I have measured out my life with coffee-spoons' is the confession from which we shrink.

What of intercession and petition? Here, too, adoration leads us to prayer which, though arising out of need, is not focused upon it. Adoration establishes us within the flow of God's love. If we are accustomed to this it becomes possible to allow ourselves to be with our distress, with the Lord: we bring ourselves in our pain to him, keeping our sight on his goodness. Or we will to do so. So much of this kind of prayer involves simply being present to God in our incapacity to be and to feel what we feel we 'should' be and feel, knowing that this – and nothing else – is what we must be, where we must be, and accepting the sense of stupidity which arises. Our willingness to be there in our helplessness without turning in on ourselves is the most forceful expression of God's primacy and of our desire for him: it is the most insistent plea for help.

What follows from this way of understanding prayer is that there is no 'higher' way, and no necessary inferiority in prayer which is primarily petition. What is all-important is that it should be directing us most fully to God, weaning us away from the demands and needs of the ego. Thus petition which springs from a deep consciousness of eating from God's hand, and which is content to remain there, more effectively dethrones ego than the silent prayer which may be giving rise to a sense of spiritual achievement.

True prayer marginalizes the ego by establishing God-in-himself at the centre of our being. Anything in prayer which works against this is inimical to the self, though fostering ego. This can happen through weakness, as in need-dominated petition, but is also found more subtly whenever prayer begins to bring with it any kind of satisfaction; whenever, from it, an individual begins to develop a persona as a 'spiritual' or 'prayerful' person. It is all too easy for the person who begins to take God and prayer seriously to slide into taking himself or herself seriously, and to fashion the ego as spiritual expert or sage. This is a very dangerous state to be in, for frequently very great gifts of mind and spirit are thus appropriated to the ego, and the resulting edifice belies the shaky foundations. This is the extreme case, but the temptation is there for all of us, adapted to our personality and situation. Our only resource in such temptation is to return to God as the Giver whatever happens to us in prayer and to refuse to label our experiences, whether joyful or painful, in ways which lend us any semblance of grandeur.

This same principle of relinquishing our experience applies in another form to the question of discussing our prayer-life and of the place of reticence. My natural inclination has been to accept (readily) the notion of 'reserve' in talking about spiritual life, out of a sense of the greatness of God and as a safeguard against the kind of familiarity which exalts ego by claiming special privilege. Nowadays I would still shrink generally from a too-easy sharing which demeans God, but I see also the danger in too great a reserve. This can itself lead to feelings of possession and uniqueness in possession: this is my spiritual goody, not for common consumption, not available to all of us; or, conversely, this woundedness is a private matter, a special affliction which makes me different, for good or ill. Thus is ego bolstered, through appropriation of God's gifts as an individually possessed commodity. Appropriate sharing of any experience or insight can disabuse us of any false sense of uniqueness and ownership, provided it is done with this intention. Our guideline for sharing should be the pattern of life of those early monastic novices who were to manifest everything about their spiritual lives to their spiritual father: the person who seeks God must own *nothing*

This became clear to me after a long period of spiritual direction in which I found it impossible to be simple and direct about myself, my experiences and my thinking, because I felt that my director would fall off his chair with laughter at the sheer incongruity of simultaneous talk about myself and God. I tied both of us up in knots trying not to say what I had to say, or to find what I thought was less high-flown language, or to wrap up those things of which I was ashamed. It took time to realize that the basis for such constraint was egotism: I was still believing that to speak of any experience was to make a claim about the worthiness of my attributes and still wanting, quite literally, to 'keep to myself' the weakness that curled me up in shame. I had to learn that neither the gifts nor the frailty were my unique possession and that to speak freely of the lavishness and gratuitousness of God to those who are nothing is to exalt him, and to deny ego gratification.

If prayer is making ourselves consciously available to God we may begin, perhaps, to see a way of fulfilling St Paul's injunction to pray always. We cannot spend our whole time in periods of exclusive, deliberate attention to God but we can train our attention Godwards, developing within ourselves a God-filled rather than an ego-filled awareness. And so the

28

corollary of any formal prayer is the practice of what is called either 'recollection' or 'mindfulness'. Mindfulness is best understood as a 'fasting' from the preoccupations and distractions of our ego through learning to be present in the one activity which engages us in the 'now'. It is often called recollection partly because it involves the drawing together of our faculties upon one activity, in contrast to their usual dissipation in numerous things which interest, worry or amuse us and so prevent our total availability to the present moment.

As you are reading this, just stop and try to be aware of all the thoughts going through your head now – 'Five minutes before picking up the kids from school', 'Why did I let that awful woman put me down?', 'I must put a new bulb in the bathroom' – and what your body is doing: fiddling with your hair, twiddling a scrap of paper. Much of our mental life involves inner chatter. Some of it reflects the too-busy lives we lead (and the egotism of trying to do and be everything to everyone); some of it, unconsciously, reflects the desire to buffer ourselves against awareness of ourselves, our situation and God. We chat to ourselves to keep ourselves company because we do not wish to face in the silence our absence from God. We want to avoid our status as capacities for God, waiting to receive him. If I stop my talk or my daydream of a glorious future or a rosy past, or abandon my dwelling on bitter memories of how hurt I have been, I am alone with the emptiness of my own existence and the pain of being 'in the land of unlikeness'. But I also make myself open to the God who says not 'I WAS' but 'I AM', the God of the living, the God of the here-and-now.

If I allow my consciousness to remain a clutter of daydreams, memories and trivia, if I allow myself to be immersed in the mindlessness within and the mindlessness without from the media, I cannot be mindful of the truths of my existence. I become increasingly trapped in the illusions of my own ego or the illusions fed to me by TV or radio programmes, books, advertising, or I become trapped in painful memories or wishful thinking, establishing an idealized image of myself as victim, saviour or whatever else takes my fancy. I become extremely successful in avoiding the present moment, worshipping either ephemera or a fossilized memory.

29

In this state I liken myself to a dog with access to a garden full of buried, old and well-chewed bones. Whenever I am low, and powerful memories of past painful or humiliating events seem to be taking over, I discover that the root cause is the desire to flee from the apparent spiritual tedium of the present, echoing Vladimir's sentiments in *Waiting for Godot*:

> All I know is that the hours are long, . . . and constrain us to beguile them with proceedings which – how shall I say? – which may seem reasonable, until they become a habit.

Sooner than face the absence, sooner than face the truth of there being nothing spectacular to force my awareness of God, no new juicy bone on offer, I run away and dig up a few old bones of old memories to gnaw. Time passes, I affirm my old depressive view of myself and the world, that is of my ego, and avoid encounter with God when my true desire is for him. In this temptation now I remember the words of the angel in St Luke's Gospel: 'Why are you looking among the dead for the One who is alive?' and set myself, however falteringly, to fast from my bones.

Such 'fasting' has negative and positive aspects; it involves refusing to engage with the memories and daydreams which present themselves to us but it also involves the positive development of the habit of attending to the present, so that we are content to give ourselves to the activity in hand and then to pass on to the next, without worrying about it beforehand and frightening ourselves into flight with the prospect of all that waits to be done. Gradually, we may become in this way simpler, more unified, and more able to do what we must do without undue reflection on ourselves in the process. In this way, although we have drawn our faculties inwards, it is, in fact, in order to turn our attention outwards, away from concentration on the mental and emotional life of the ego.

As this habit develops, when an activity is not all-engrossing we may not automatically fall back into ego-dominated chatter, daydream or memory. Are we left, then, with mental vacancy? This would, indeed, be mindlessness. No, mindfulness implies an object for our attention, a focus: when it is not the task in hand then it is to be God, the God of revelation, the God of Scripture. To develop mindfulness, while refusing domination by painful memories, it is essential to store our minds with all that reminds us of him.

'Mindfulness' and 'recollection' both suggest 'presence of mind' and 'memory'. If we recollect or are mindful of someone, we bring memory of them into our present consciousness. So mindfulness of God involves us in cultivating the memory of who God is and what he has done for us. It means making the knowledge and praise of God given through Scripture, and to a lesser extent, through his holy men and women, our basic mental furniture. In this way the positive recollection of the mighty works of God combats our ego, with its selected memories of its own experience.

We see these two types of memory operating clearly in the experience of the Jews of the Old Testament. Jewish faith is based on memory of what the Lord has done in the covenant relationship with his people. We see this, for example, in the harvest thanksgiving formula found in Deuteronomy 26:5–9. Thanks for present mercies begin in recollection of the Jews' origins and deliverance from Egypt: 'My father was a wandering Aramaean. He went down into Egypt, to find refuge there, few in numbers; . . .' Whenever they replaced this mindfulness of God's actions and call with memories arising out of the desires and needs of their egos, disaster ensued, as they discovered in the desert: oh for the flesh-pots of Egypt! The desire of the ego for satisfaction, warmth, food, security, rest – all necessary – may lead to delusive memory which falsifies the past. Its end is idolatry, quite literally for the Israelites in the desert, metaphorically for us now, in the creation, through such memory, of false goals, false self-images, false visions of reality. The novelist Charles Dickens was keenly aware of this duality in our power of memory; one novel and one short story have proved very useful in fleshing-out just what this idea may mean in our experience.

In Dickens's short story *The Haunted Man*, Redfearn, the central character, is dogged by agonizing memories which lead him to make a pact with the devil for the removal altogether of his memory. The consequence is, of course, that he disintegrates. He can no longer sustain any relationship because he has no recollection of the bonds which unite him

31

to others, of the love which he has received from them. Moreover, Dickens insists, the worst aspect of this loss is that
Redfearn has no memory of Christ and his redemptive work,
no awareness of himself as a being both requiring and having
received redemption. He has no one to whom he can give
thanks as source and redeemer. He has become, in fact, pure
ego, living to and from himself, with no awareness of dependence upon, or derivation from, God and others. Like Mil-
ton's Satan he discovers that 'Myself am Hell' and discloses
to us the necessity of cultivating Godward, thankful memory.

In *Great Expectations* we are shown in the character of Miss
Havisham the way in which ego-centred memory may lead
to the idolatry of a false self-image. Jilted on her wedding
day, Miss Havisham freezes time at that instant, refusing to
admit the passage of time and maintaining her house as a
mausoleum for her thwarted hopes. Her entire life thence-
forward centres on that memory of treachery and on the image
of herself as an innocent victim. Her life and the lives of those
with whom she is involved must serve only to maintain this
image: she makes of herself an idol to whom satisfaction must
be paid. She becomes, therefore, both an idol and a figure of
death-in-life: false memory has made her akin to the vampire,
sucking life from the present and the living, in order to sustain
a moment from the past. Salvation only comes to her when
she can use her memory to respond to the immediate reality
of another person, to step outside ego by allowing memory to
kindle awareness of a common humanity. How often do we,
likewise, meet people whose lives are invested in being, for
example, bereaved, and who have locked themselves and their
families into continual observance of their condition as mourn-
ers? How often do we find in ourselves reluctance to respond
to a new situation or a new person, because we are caught
in a 'time-warp' from a similar situation which continues to
dominate our expectations and our behaviour?

Dickens's mind was formed in part by Scripture so that the
great themes of the incarnation and the redemption form the
bases for his greatest novels, while scriptural references are
apparently unconsciously interwoven into his prose. If we,
too, are to deny ego through mindfulness we need a similar
immersion in Scripture, and a new way of reading. Most of

us have several ways of reading: for pleasure we may well skim read, perhaps reading the end first, or omitting chunks which seem dull or irrelevant. For study we may skim in a different way, 'filleting' a text for the main issues; or read slowly, making notes, analysing and arguing as we go. Reading as a corollary of prayer and recollection requires yet another approach. The intention is to provide neither pleasure nor information but to allow the Word of God to take root in us and to read us, to search us out over time. This kind of reading asks us to linger with a passage, perhaps even a line, or a word, which evokes a response in us, and to let this rest in our minds without trying to analyse or argue with it. We must learn to stay with the passage and to brood over it during the day, letting it form the background music for our consciousness at unoccupied moments.

Our ego constantly tries to master words and ideas, to control and organize them into something it can use. This kind of reading allows the words to master us, in much the same way as my week spent in prayer before the Mother and Child icon produced in me ideas of which I had not been consciously aware and which had not been worked upon by reason. If this idea still seems strange, another way of understanding it is by comparison with the times when a tune has suddenly taken up residence in your head and you have been unable to stop hearing it. This kind of reading accepts this tendency of the mind to bring into consciousness what has been heard and recorded: it accepts that, as with the computer, it is a case of 'garbage in, garbage out'. It ensures that the 'music' you thus hear turns your attention Godward rather than towards the ego-centred memories evoked by our other mental 'noise'.

To cultivate this kind of immersion in Scripture, familiarity, far from breeding contempt, is essential. Familiarity with the same translation, with the same group of readings, the same psalms, the same rite in our worship, builds up our positive mindfulness. So, too, does the committing to memory of psalms, prayers and scripture passages: when our attention is not required by immediate tasks these words, which transcend our ego, may then fill our awareness when we are unable to remain still and silent for God. Furthermore the lack of excitement, the lack of novelty of the familiar is another means of withdrawing sustenance from the ego, which is always looking to the new as an escape from the apparent tediousness of the present moment. To learn to stay with what is familiar, to listen deeply to it and dig beneath its surface is to affirm the self's orientation towards Christ who is for us now, but yet is the same yesterday, today and for ever.

Fasting from ego may include, of course, fasting from food. This fast must not be thought of as an attempt to punish our bodies as though they, and not our ego, are responsible for sin. Fasting, rather, affirms the involvement of our bodies in our selfhood, the integrated spirit-soul-body. Our turning to God involves and uses our bodies which were created to give him glory. It is egotism which frequently leads to the denial of the body, for ego so often tends to refuse the constraints of embodiedness and to claim distinctiveness from the rest of creation.

The origin for our fast must be Jesus' statement that his disciples will fast when the bridegroom is taken from them. Experiencing physical hunger is a powerful means of making real to ourselves our hunger for God and our refusal to replace him with anything created. It also highlights the 'eschatological tension' in our selfhood: we do not have the bridegroom with us in all his fullness; we must wait, hungering and thirsting, for his final coming. We must be content to wait with our emptiness, with the pain of our unmet need for the One who can satisfy us. Thus it may mean that, though there may be times of greater intensity of fasting, the basic fast from food for us is the daily small restriction of our intake which prevents us ever feeling entirely satisfied.

Periods of more intense fasting, or simply the adoption of an older approach which excluded all our now usual snacks, also expose the triviality, the flight from reality and the domination of the needs of our ego in our lives. I am certainly aware of how much eating can be for me a means to fill in time, to avoid facing the blank page in front of me or the blank spirit when I should be praying or meeting the person who expects what I feel unable to give. How endless days can seem when fasting! The rituals with which we rightly sur-

34

round eating can so often become supports to our ego, ways of controlling and organizing time so that unpleasant awareness is reduced, just as overeating in itself may make us soporific and able to pass the day in minimal response.

There is, however, a double edge to fasting from food or from anything which feeds our ego. Because it is our own undertaking it is fatally easy to fall into the trap of focusing on success and failure in such a way that the service of ego, and not of God, becomes our objective. I recall with horror the section in that influential book *A Celebration of Discipline* which spoke of increasing our efforts once 'we have fasted with a degree of spiritual success'. Such an approach robs fasting of its very purpose of opening us up to God, with its encouragement to develop through it a feeling of satisfaction and an image of ourselves as 'spiritual' people. When any action we undertake seems inclined to bring us spiritual kudos it is far better to stop it, changing to a less satisfying method of attending to God, or to bring awareness of the temptation immediately before God, so that the illusion of our 'expertise' or success is dissolved in the acceptance of our frailty. We need to remember the story of St Francis of Assisi who retired one Lent with a number of bread rolls, to fast in commemoration of Christ's fast. On his return one roll was found half-eaten. The untouched bread, he said, was in honour of the Lord, the half-eaten roll a guard against vainglory.

One of the fullest ways in which we can live this fast from ego is to accept the ordinariness of ourselves and our lives. By 'ordinary' I do not mean – as the word is so often misunderstood – mediocre. Nor do I mean ordinary in that we do not see the full dimensions of full Christian life. What I do mean by it is the acceptance of whatever befalls us in our everyday life as the work God intends for us, as the way he chooses for us to meet him. It means not looking for special experiences and not looking for special ways of serving God which neglect those to whom we owe our everyday love and care. It can be very flattering to the ego to be the 'listening ear' for everyone in trouble, the 'open door' to those who make us feel a worthwhile, wise and 'mature' Christian. The true self then suffers from what appears to be a living-out of the second great commandment but is in fact a form of ego-

35

idolatry, making others dependent on us while abandoning to their own devices those whose less spectacular needs make legitimate demands on us. This is by no means to advocate insularity: I wish simply to stress that seeing caring for others and being prayerful as part of the *ordinary* life of all Christians may save us from this trap. This is a theme common to novelists and spiritual guides. Listen to what that great guide, Jean-Nicolas Grou, has to say on the first effects of conversion:

> Neglect of business and duties under a pretext of piety is a fairly common fault. Devotees . . . often fall into this error, and so give scandal – it is not piety that is to blame but rather the self-will which is followed instead of the Spirit of God. Many have no sooner taken up the practices of religion than they neglect their homes, children and those dependent on them. They spend the day going to Church, in running after popular preachers . . . and undertaking all manner of good works. They are to be found everywhere except at home, which they leave as early and return to as late as possible. Meanwhile, all is disorder in the household; everyone does as he pleases in the absence of the mistress. Children are left to the doubtful care of those who themselves want looking after; or they are dragged about, especially if they are girls, from service to service, until they are wearied out and disgusted, and soon begin to tire of religion. The husband very rightly complains, but his word is not heeded, and he is secretly accused of not being sufficiently devout.
>
> And thus it is too with many men. They are active, bustling busybodies; meddling in everything under the pretext of serving God; fancying that the Church depends on them. They concern themselves with the affairs of others, and neglect their own.
>
> In all religious exercises not of strict obligation (piety) bids us accommodate ourselves to the wishes and frailty of those whom we are bound to consider, and for the sake of peace, to sacrifice our own tastes, be they never so pious.

Dickens puts this into a frequently more comic perspective in his novel *Bleak House*. The redoubtable Mrs Jellyby is hailed as a great woman for her indefatigable labours on behalf of the unevangelized people of Borrioboola-Gha. But, in her ego-inflating zeal, Mrs Jellyby can see nothing of the ordinary distress among the poor of London, the homeless street-sweepers, the vagrant children. Nor can she see the hopelessness and chaos at the heart of her own home, which is too small, too unspectacular to command her interest. As Dickens tartly remarks of her response to a street boy:

> He is not softened by distance and unfamiliarity . . . he is not a genuine foreign-grown savage; he is the ordinary home-grown article . . . Homely filth begrimes him, homely parasites devour him, homely sores are in him, homely rags are on him: native ignorance, the growth of English soil and climate, sinks his immortal nature lower than the beasts that perish.

We have all, doubtless, known such people; we all, I am sure, recognize the tendency in ourselves. When the gospel seems to ask for extravagant gestures – the apostles leaving their nets immediately they are called, the rich man being asked to sell all – and when Christian history seems to be the story of those who have loved through extravagant gestures – St Francis of Assisi, St Anthony the Great – it is difficult to remember that Jesus also spent thirty years of his life as a quite ordinary, unremarkable artisan, without even the special quality of poverty. We need to learn to live the radical dispossession asked of us by the gospel in this unassuming way. The self that is being conformed to Christ through the denial of ego is called to reflect the totality of Christ whose ordinariness as a working man gave scandal when he proclaimed that in him the liberating power of God was manifest (Luke 4:16–30). There is hope here for those who feel enmeshed in suburbia, in a humdrum pattern of work and family life: we are, indeed, sometimes asked to give this up for a less outwardly secure and settled existence, but more often than not we are asked to go more deeply into it, to allow ourselves to be hidden by the ordinariness of our lives while active in dispossessing ourselves of all that is not God. We must keep in mind that Nazareth is 'the gospel lived before being proclaimed' (Mère Marie-Thérèse Dubouché) and ponder on the words of St Francis de Sales:

Cling to your lowliness as the bond of your worth, practise humility generously in the might of him who accomplished his greatest works in the humiliation of the cross.

Be ever lowly and daily become more lowly in your own eyes . . . How great is this littleness! . . . then the Son of God could find in you some likeness to himself, some reproduction of his interior life, poor and common in the sight of men, but rich and fruitful in the sight of God.

Fasting from ego in this way also implies adopting the same attitude to others as we do to God, of giving our whole attention to the other while holding at arm's length our own thoughts, needs, daydreams. Anyone who has been taught the basics of listening in counselling will know that in essence we are required to be attentively receptive: to hear without judgement and to reflect back accurately what we have heard. We are, in fact, adopting a prayerful attitude before the mystery of the person which we can only do if we have ceased, even if merely for that time, to hear the 'noise' of our own opinions, our own judgements, our own experiences. A helpful kind of 'fast' may well be to identify and refrain from one of those habits which defend us from the reality of the other: the need to dominate or withdraw in conversation, to make the wisecrack or silly remark which refuses intimacy, to insist upon intensity and profundity when the other needs simply to rest in us. We all know ways in which we pad ourselves against the impact of others, refusing their and our humanity.

It is this kind of awareness of the person as 'the Temple of the Shekinah', as Thomas Carlyle puts it, the dwelling-place of God's glory, which brings the concept of 'vigil' into our everyday life. We need to develop a vigilance, an alertness to the needs of the other and the ways in which they are calling us to fulfil gospel precepts. It is one of the glories of St Benedict's monastic rule that he helps us to see mutual love as mutual obedience: to love someone is to find ways in which we can do things in their way rather than in ours, without idolizing their needs or producing dependency. This is one way of loving others as ourselves. Going the extra mile may mean quietly carrying out the other's neglected share of practical jobs at home as well as providing emotional support during a time of stress or overwork. Imitating the giving of the poor widow's mite may be being the one to get up to tend the crying child in the night when both of you as parents feel at the end of your tether and unable to face the coming day. We have to be alert to all the opportunities for loving, practically, which are offered to us during the day. Once again our attention is being trained away from ourselves, our egos, towards the realities of love.

Living in this state of alertness enables us to fulfil more often the two great commandments and to appreciate their unity. As we grow free from ego we not only grow free to share in the life of God but also in the lives of others whom we recognize to be equally images of God, equally destined to be 'sons in the Son'. And so gradually the barriers begin to be broken down so that we recognize in the vagrant, the addict, all those we do not consider 'respectable' – yes, the asset-stripping financier and rapacious entrepreneur, too, a son of God and doubly a 'brother'; a brother in sharing creation as an image of God and sharing in creaturely nothingness without him.

'Knowing of what we are made' alters, too, our attitude towards creation. At the moment it is fashionable to be 'green', to reacknowledge the fragility of the eco-system and our responsibility to it. I want to consider it in another way. In the incarnation Christ took the dust of the earth into God: it is intended to be filled with his glory, as are our embodied selves which come from it. Yet creation too, as St Paul tells us, is, like us, held in bondage, looking for the end-time. When we live with our total being towards God we are taking creation with us, joining in its groaning in labour. We become doubly aware that our life is not lived for ourselves but towards God, in and for others, in and for the whole creation. The final state of cosmic transfiguration, of unity between our selves and creation, in an experience of tenderness and joy, is evoked for us in one of the closing chapters of George MacDonald's last, greatest, novel *Lilith*:

Every growing thing showed me, by its shape and colour, the indwelling idea – the informing thought, that is, which was its being and sent it out. My bare feet seemed to love every plant they trod upon. The world and my being, its life and mine, were one. The microcosm and the macrocosm were at length at-oned, at length in harmony! I lived in everything and everything entered and lived in me. To be aware of a thing, was to know its life at once and mine, to know whence we came, and where we were at home – was to know that we are all what we are, because Another is what he is! Sense after sense, hitherto asleep, awoke in me . . .

. . . See every little flower straighten its stalk, lift up its neck, and with outstretched head stand expectant: something more than the sun, greater than the light, is coming, is coming – none the less surely coming that it is long upon the road! What matters today, or tomorrow, or ten thousand years to Life himself, to Love himself! He is coming, is coming, and the necks of all humanity are stretched out to see him come! . . . When he comes, will he indeed find us watching thus?

4

Selfhood, solidarity and intercession

'When you gain a brother, you gain God'

The picture we have just been given in *Lilith* is a picture of harmony, of a unity between humanity and the earth which foreshadows unity between God and the human race. This unity is the vocation, the calling, of each self, who is made to reflect Christ, the reconciler of all things in heaven and earth, so that we might live to the praise of the Father's glory (Ephesians 1:10–11). To live to the Father's glory is to live as his children; sons and daughters after the image of the Son, Jesus. If we are to be our full selves, fully human beings, then we must live in recognition of this relationship of child to parent. We do not simply live towards God as our source, as our Creator, but towards him as one who loves us into being. As George MacDonald puts it, we are not so much the work of God's hands as the offspring of his heart. To become aware of God's love for us is, then, to begin to realize the existence of spiritual bonding; 'sonship', what the mystic Jacob Boehme called 'childship', is at the heart of our existence.

If we are, then, 'sons and daughters' through our very existence as images of Christ, it must follow that the bonds which unite us to the Father also unite us, in our being, to one another. Our brotherhood and sisterhood in Christ is as real and as ineluctable as our relationships within our families: as in our families we have not chosen our brothers and sisters, so in our familial relationship with God we cannot choose him as our Father, nor choose to live as though we are brothers and sisters. We can simply choose to live out or deny what God has made us.

This may sound like a woolly universalism which rejects the need for personal relationship with Christ, for personal recognition of Christ's saving work taking place for us and in us. Far from it. We must become, in actuality, what God has made it possible for us to become. Christ's sacrifice 'for all' must not remain a vague universal but be made specific, fully accepted by each one of us. Our 'conversion', however, whether it be the slow working of grace or the sudden moment of revelation and commitment, is not a choice of God as Father and Jesus as Saviour and Brother, as though they were now ours and we were removed from the common destiny of the human race. Rather, conversion is our consent to the Holy Spirit's activating the spirit of sonship within us, making us, as Irenaeus says, sons not simply by virtue of our creation but also, like Jesus, through willed obedience to the Father. Thus, the experience of sonship of which the Christian is conscious may be heightened to such an intensity that it seems of a different order to that of his non-believing brother or sister, while remaining in reality a gift from the same source. Christians may be seen, perhaps, as those who allow the gift to be fulfilled in them, on behalf of their brothers and sisters. We must preach and teach personal Christianity, a Christianity which asks a response from the whole of us to the totality of God, but if we understand our selfhood as binding us to all, we will not preach an individualistic Christianity, in which God 'saves' us as individual units. As F. D. Maurice so often repeated, we must preach God's intention to make of us 'a royal priesthood, a holy nation' (1 Peter 2:9).

We can say, then, that sonship and brotherhood are written into us, name us, give us our identity. Brotherhood does not, however, mean sameness, being identical. Each self is a particular image of Christ the Brother; it shares in family likeness, shares in the same characteristics, looks to the same source, knows the same bonds and yet remains unique. We offend against our brotherhood when we live as individuals, refusing relationship, but we equally offend when we demand that others be clones, all manifesting identical behaviour, interests and approaches to life. How often do we find, both in the natural family and the church family, a plea for brotherhood which is, in reality, a form of coercion into uniformity? How often in church and social life does the concept of brotherhood decline into an excuse for excluding the outsider, or for laying down conditions of acceptance into fellowship? Too often the rhetoric of brotherhood, shorn of its Christian meaning, leads to a totalitarian spirit, which is outwardly based on apprehension of bonding but is inwardly a consequence of individualism.

The individualist believes that his or her personality is the guarantor of his or her uniqueness and independence; others may then be experienced as threatening to that distinctiveness. They must then either be rigorously excluded by a narrow focusing on their distinguishing traits or adopted as 'second selves' to be fitted into the ego's pre-existing mould. The emphasis on brotherhood is then a means of projecting the ego of the strongest group member onto all.

In the collectivist vision of brotherhood, on the other hand, only the group is admitted as possessing a separate identity. Flight from personal consciousness leads to the emergence of a group ego, so that personal identity and the personal struggle between self and ego is left unacknowledged and undeveloped. This is not 'brotherhood', for no distinctive brothers and sisters are allowed to exist!

Christian brotherhood, rooted in belief in our identity as images of Christ the Son, helps us to avoid the traps of individualism and collectivism. With it we are not threatened by the distinctiveness of ourselves and others but neither are we seduced by the vision of individuality into recognizing as 'kin' only those whose ego-attributes correspond with ours or appeal to our personalities as attractive, vulnerable or responsive to us. Christian brotherhood enables us to see ourselves as belonging to, and with, all others; to know that we share with them both our divine inheritance as a son of God and the unloveliness of the Prodigal Son among his pigs, and that we owe one another both reverence and the fellowship so often uniting beggars.

Christian brotherhood, therefore, implies that we see one another whole, that we can pay them the honour of

43

acknowledging the darkness, the woundedness, the despair and the capacity for evil that is in them because we know it is in us, and that God has not flinched from being part of it. When we can do this, our brothers and sisters cease to be either the dustbin for all those rejected unacceptable aspects of ourselves, or heroes and heroines who must fulfil all our aspirations by proxy, as a repository for all the goodness lacking in ourselves. The true grasp of brotherhood is a powerful antidote to the fantasies about ourselves and others which so hinder our responsiveness to God and to our brothers and sisters.

Living in brotherhood, like living in humility, implies living in the truth of our being; it is closely linked to humility for it involves us in knowing of what we are made, and in knowing that in the gratuitous gift of our selfhood comes the gift of our brothers and sisters. We are made to be gifts to one another, gifts to be welcomed, gifts to be valued for what they are. We do not judge a gift but neither do we use a silk dress for washing the floor or set a lump of coal on the dresser as an ornament. We must, as brothers, treat our brothers-as-gifts similarly, acknowledging their frailty, expressed in ways different to ours, but also confronting them gently with their truth when it is necessary. Brotherly love is, in this way, frequently tough-minded. It may mean enabling the brother to see what is not brotherly and sonlike in his own actions by speaking the truth in love: it may mean, at times, outright opposition to his aims. What characterizes all our behaviour in these situations, however, when we act from our selfhood, is that we never see our opponent as alien, as someone without claims on us. Enemies are always estranged brothers; while we need to recognize the hostility that lies between us we also need to recognize the state of inner hostility within us, for where there is discord between brothers our selfhood is wounded. The bombing of the Conservative conference at Brighton in 1985 brought this home to me starkly. The day before that bomb incident I remember indulging in what I glibly called righteous indignation, calling down a plague upon the whole house of politicians of whatever persuasion. For the moment all politicians had become, not brothers and sisters struggling with their good intentions alongside their egotistical pretensions and weaknesses, but a sub-human grouping subject to my judgement and condemnation. The next day came the murder and maiming of some of these same people. The full destructive power of the denial of brotherhood hurt me most forcibly: those who planted the bombs had given physical reality to that denial and had assumed godlike powers to punish and to take life.

Brotherly love is accepting love, then, but it is truthful love, true to the reality of our creation in God's image and to the reality of our loss of it. And such truth is part of the healing brought about by brotherhood, as witnessed by the founders of the French lay community 'Pain de Vie' (Bread of Life). Founded on a life of Eucharist-centred prayer the community, many of whom have been drug-addicts and 'drop-outs', shares its life with those who are similarly 'marginal', addicts and alcoholics, the mentally ill, the criminal. It has no 'programme' of therapy apart from the regular life of prayer and relationship in the community, which involves reflecting and receiving the truth about ourselves. As Pascal Pingault, their founder, says:

> We have learnt, in living with poor people, that it is extremely important to tell each person the truth about his state. Love for the poor must not be made into sentimentality: no soft-centred mystical feelings!
>
> A young girl whom we had welcomed right at the start, deeply wounded by repeated suicide attempts, had quickly regained her appetite for life with us. She became so happy that she wanted to take on a responsible post in the community. But she had damaged her hips, she had damaged her brain, her hands had become useless; it was impossible. 'No, you cannot do that work now. First learn to iron your clothes, to look after yourself. You can at least do that yourself; you have lost the habit of doing these daily jobs.' She was truly full of illusions, she dreamed a lot. Her past was rooted in her memory and she refused to face her present-day reality . . . Today she is well.

Here brotherly love involved sharing the pain of speaking and acting upon hard and hurtful truth. So often we refuse to face with others such realities, believing we are acting out of brotherly concern when, in fact, we are trying to avoid the pain of relationship: pain in seeing another's hurt, pain in being experienced as the one who inflicts such hurt. To love as a brother involves us in being for others, being attached, related to them, but detached from the needs of our own egos.

It is in the light of this concept of the self as brother, I think, that we begin to understand more fully Jesus' commandment to 'love one another as I have loved you'. Jesus loves us as son and brother, loves us because God has chosen a filial relationship for us. Jesus' love flows from him to us because of the relationship existing between us. Love is the expression of that relationship; it is no arbitrary decision. The commandment to love, then, is no more than the injunction 'be yourself'; love for our brothers and sisters is not the response to an arbitrary demand of God but the consequence of living what we are.

Once we have begun to see the commandment to love in this way we start also to reinterpret that much-debased word 'duty' as a corollary of love. From the viewpoint of our ego, dominated by the instinct for self-preservation and self-assertion, 'duty', whether the duty of worshipping God or the duty to care for others, appears as an imposition, a demand from without which goes against the grain of our nature. An action performed out of duty is frequently opposed negatively to one performed spontaneously. Doing what we want to do is seen as preferable to actions undertaken without any gratification on our part. How often have you heard agnostics argue against a God who demands worship? To them the duty of worship is a requirement of God extraneous to our nature. Similarly, how often do you hear people complain about 'duty calls' on relatives? To them the duties arising from their family relationships are experienced as in opposition to their self-expression, as limits on their individual freedom.

If we consider duty from the viewpoint of our childship and brotherhood we gain a different perspective. Duty is derived from the Latin term which gives us words like debt, owe and ought. To fulfil our duty is simply to respond according to our spiritual nature, to what is evoked by those to whom we are related, to what that person is. The duty to worship arises thus from the recognition of God, of his love, his goodness, his beauty and his desire for us. As a creature I have a duty of worship because God is who he is and I am who I am: I acknowledge fact and live as a dependent creature. As a child of God I have a duty of worship because I recognize with love and awe the God who has loved me into being and sustains me by that love: I affirm the reality of the love-relationship in my spirit's natural response of worship. Fulfilment of this duty is part and parcel of my true self-fulfilment, although to my ego, with its desire for centrality, such duty feels a painful, unnecessary demand. Similarly, I have a duty of brotherly, sisterly love because I recognize the relationship existing between persons. To do my duty to another is to acknowledge what one child and brother owes to another and is owed in turn: fulfilling my duty to my brothers and sisters affirms and nurtures both my identity and theirs.

The conflict which we saw in earlier chapters as that between self and ego we can see also as that between brotherhood and individualism. The ego which declares itself 'a self-made man' disregards not only derivation from and relationship to God, but also his similar bonds to others. In the early chapters of Genesis the breaking of the bond with God is soon followed by the sin of Cain, the breaking of the bond with the brother. The temptation to become as gods, by our doing, is swiftly followed by the disclaimer 'Am I my brother's keeper?': autonomy with regard to God leads us to claim the same untrammelled freedom in human relationships.

To the great Anglican theologian William Law this defiance of bonding was the root of our human sinfulness. In his understanding, the biblical drama of reprobation and salvation was recapitulated in every person. In each of us our spiritual self, our imaging of Christ, is the just man Abel who affirms bonding, while our ego is Cain the destroyer of human bonds in defiance of God. The work of fasting from ego, of dying to it, is the battle of Abel to withstand Cain: the wages of sin are death because in sin, the choice of ego over God, Cain the destroyer of brotherhood is triumphant, as murderer of our selfhood.

This vision of our inner battle between Cain and Abel has, of course, its relevance to our social life. Where individualism is the dominant strain in social and political thinking and policy, Cain may be said to be in the ascendant in our national life and we open ourselves to a condition of 'all against all' in an egotistic scramble for individual survival and self-betterment. The 'prophet of Chelsea', Thomas Carlyle, perceived this as the reality of his own Victorian age, an age in which 'the sacrament of marriage', that is, the spiritual bonding between persons, had been replaced by 'the sacrament of divorce'. Carlyle illustrated his point with the story of the Irish widow (and in his day who could be lower socially?) dying from typhus-fever and being denied, not only help, but any recognition of her sisterhood. Sisterhood 'in the bone' nevertheless asserts itself, for from her infection these rejecting brothers also die. Is there not equally a moral here for our own age, in which the existence of social bonds is frequently denied, while at the same time we are sometimes terror-stricken by the awareness of our physical interdependence: does not the reality of AIDS and of contamination from nuclear accidents write large for us, in our day, our brotherhood in the bone? Should it not also alert us to our brotherhood in spirit?

There are, of course, many signs of hope, especially in the growth of new communities and new perspectives on social life coming from those who live with the least respected and least valued in our western society – people who are mentally handicapped, and mentally ill, people who are addicted to drugs, alcohol, gambling, people who are suffering from AIDS, people who are rootless, homeless, hopeless. Communities such as Jean Vanier's 'l'Arche' and the many, unknown, families who have received a mentally handicapped child as their own, point us towards the possibility of building a community based on brotherhood, and witness to brotherhood in the Body of Christ as a way which brings healing and harmony. Listen again to the experience of the Community of the Bread of Life:

> Our welcome is unconditional in the sense that it is not specialized. A people is formed of every kind of individual

48

and it is a people that we have been called to form, a people bringing together every vocation, a eucharistic people of whom the poor are an integral part . . . Man was not made to live alone. He must live as a member of a Body. And the poor person, to be healed, must know that he belongs to a people and that he will never be excluded from it, on any pretext . . . It is this which enables him to withstand in his heart the greatest sufferings. To live this Communion, this alliance, to know it is true! Whether one be the most inveterate alcoholic or someone utterly disintegrated mentally, healing itself matters little when one has encountered that! Doesn't fundamental healing have its source in the unshakable conviction of being grafted, and for all eternity, into a Body drawn by God? It is together that we will become saints, each of us absolutely indispensable to the other . . . It is in this way that we welcome the poor, the marginalized, hoping for their healing but mobilizing ourselves especially in the hope that we are moving together towards Christ. Wounds will surely remain for ever. There will remain, at least, scars. But it is with these that the Lord Jesus appeared in his glorified Body! And it is by his wounds that we are healed. It is without doubt, also, by the wounds of the most marginalized, when they are offered and cauterized, that the whole Body is sanctified.

We cannot all live this large-scale experience of community, but we can all acknowledge the inner truth of our brotherhood in a healing Body and begin to make it a reality in small ways by the way we think, feel and act towards those who live on the edge of our society, physically, mentally, morally.

I have concentrated upon the witness of the Bread of Life community because their life also exemplifies the eschatological tension which is at the heart of our brotherhood, as of our selfhood. We know, all too painfully, that we bear the image of 'the man the dust' as much as the image of the Son. In our brotherhood, as I have already suggested, we are called to live in recognition not only of our brotherhood in a glory as yet incompletely realized, but also of our brotherhood in frailty, in fallenness, in estrangement from God and captivity to Cain. To live as a brother or sister is to live in the self-knowledge which embraces the frailty, the venality, the beggarliness of the other as belonging to oneself. It is to face squarely the unloveliness and brokenness of the other and see in it one's own; to know that the violence and the desire to crush what threatens by its fragility, experienced so terrifyingly in the other, terrifies because it echoes one's own. Brotherhood makes us know, through and through, that the message of Revelation 3:17–18 is for every one of us:

> You say to yourself, 'I am rich, I have made a fortune, and have everything I want', never realizing that you are wretchedly and piteously poor, and blind and naked, too. I warn you, buy from me the gold that has been tested in the fire to make you really rich, and white robes to clothe you and cover your nakedness, and eye ointment to put on your eyes so that you are able to see.

It is only from the communion of sinners that there can be any communion of saints.

This understanding of our solidarity in sin with our brothers and sisters immediately rids our love and care of any trace of guilt or paternalism. So often our motivation to care for others springs from guilt, from a need to help 'the less fortunate', which establishes us, either guiltily or proudly, as the possessors sharing our possessions with the 'deprived'. This kind of sharing is a necessary prelude to, but it is not yet, the sharing involved in brotherhood, for it still presupposes that some of us do, in justice and truth, possess the earth. True brotherhood emerges when we meet others as one beggar with another, united in confidence in the beneficence of God. The definition of evangelism as 'one beggar telling another beggar where to get bread' is also a definition of our life together as brothers and sisters. While we see ourselves as owners of whatever gifts we have received we will never see a brother or sister but only a recipient of our benevolence. Ego blinds us to ourselves and to others.

Again, the history of the Bread of Life community illustrates this truth: their vocation to welcome the marginalized into their lives of total dependence on Providence arose out of no decision to give to brothers and sisters from their wealth, spiritual or otherwise, but from awareness of their own needs before God:

> . . . we have gathered together around Jesus because we need him. We didn't go looking for the poor, they arrived! And it's thus that we gradually came into our vocation of hospitality; we had so much need ourselves of the hospitality of Christ. . . . Another difficulty in welcoming the poor rests in the fact that the poor person disturbs us. His sickness says to me: 'You, too, somewhere, feel rejected and unloved by others.' . . . To pray usefully for a poor person, do we not know that we must accept . . . that this poverty which strikes them down may also strike me down as well? Is this not the meaning of compassion, to suffer with?

I have come to appreciate this, painfully, through the long-term experience of depression, or should I say, through living through a depressive personality. During social-work training I spent some time working in a community school for disturbed, intelligent girls. On the first day I had the misfortune, in one sense, to be mistaken for an anticipated new inmate; among the other residential workers this was considered disastrous, for the régime depended on strict differentiation between girls and staff. I found this a taste of hell because I knew, at a psychological and social level, my likeness to these girls, despite differences in the ways we registered and expressed psychological poverty and distress, but also because I knew that the girls recognized this distress in all of us. They rightly accused us of hypocrisy, of being the blind leading the blind.

This identification remained for some time at the psychological level, reinforced during one bout of depression by a kind of claustrophobia which made me see a little, from the inside, of the lives of those who wander our streets with all their belongings, unable to settle, unable to relate. Much later, in a spasm of what Dr Frank Lake used to call 'hardening of the oughteries', I found this identification a sure sign of unacceptable weakness. I had been given so much, helped so much, that I ought to be strong, and whole, an 'OK person'. All these disturbed girls and wanderers should have no place in my psyche or my spiritual life. It was in this mood that I listened in church to that part of Paul's letter to the Corinthians (1 Corinthians 4:7–11) in which he compares the apostles and 'respectable Christians'. It was the reading for the wrong year and so came totally unexpectedly:

> What do you have that was not given to you? And if it was given, how can you boast as though it were not? Is it that you have everything you want – that you are rich already, in possession of your kingdom, with us left outside? Indeed I wish you were really kings, and we could be kings with you! But instead, it seems to me, God has put us apostles at the end of his parade, with the men sentenced to death; it is true – we have been put on show in front of the whole universe, angels as well as men. Here we are, fools for the sake of Christ, while you are the learned men in Christ; we have no power, but you are influential; you are celebrities, we are nobodies.

Suddenly, I felt as though overrun inside by tramps and beggars and realized that all those whom I had tried to eject from my selfhood, to make it respectable and 'virtuous', were, in fact, *me*, were mine; their rightful place was in me and I was at last free to accept my spiritual sisterhood with all those whom our culture regards as nothing and to cease despising my own nothingness.

Here again we may see the mystery of God's ways: it is through the acceptance of our brotherhood as men of dust, through the emptying of ourselves of all pretensions to possess our qualities and our gifts that we find ourselves gradually becoming conformed to Christ our brother, who poured himself out for us, taking on himself the nothingness of a slave (Philippians 2:5–8). Our acceptance of our dustiness, and our brotherhood in dust, is the only way to reach the glory of our identity as 'first-born sons' (Hebrews 12:22–25).

Such acceptance of poverty and sinfulness must finally transcend our individual responsibility. As we come to know the poverty, the fragility and woundedness of our own lives and that of our brothers and sisters, our boundaries begin to extend towards infinity. We may begin to live as selves which encompass the totality of human nature and to see that our sense of affliction, our awareness of sin and guilt is an experience of the pain of the whole Body. We do not bear the lostness and estrangement of ourselves only but of the human race; although of some things innocent in our own lives as persons we bear the burden of guilt with, and for, others. Increasingly we know ourselves to be caught up in the labour of a creation and awaiting its liberation, awaiting the revelation of the sons of God (Romans 8:15–23). Our willingness to embrace the tension of 'the already and the not yet', looking expectantly for the coming of God, makes our inner lives of fast from ego lives of a brotherhood which shares in the redemptive power of Christ's sonship and brotherhood.

Christ, the first-born of many brothers (Romans 8:29) fulfilled that brotherhood through vicariousness, by standing totally on our behalf. As St Paul says: 'For our sake God made the sinless one into sin so that in him we might become the righteousness of God' (2 Corinthians 5:21); Christ takes on himself our estrangement from God, restores us in himself to the father. Consequently, our selfhood, our brotherhood, must also be vicarious; to be a self is to be an intercessor, one who pleads for his brothers and sisters by being totally one of them.

Intercession, then, is part and parcel of true brotherhood. It is not an activity we may choose but our very being; we are made to live intercession, being one with our brothers and sisters before God, just as Jesus, our elder brother, lives for ever in heaven to intercede for us.

If we look at intercession and 'on behalfness' in this way, then they lose the connotations of superiority which sometimes accompany them. We can only truly be before, within, God on behalf of others when we know the truth of 'I in them and they in me'. In being before God in my wretchedness, my sin, my fragility, I bring all my brothers and sisters to him. Intercession does not make me a 'go-between' raised above the mess and muddle of human life, but buries me deeply within it so that when I am exposed to God it is all taken with me. When I live as a simple capacity for God then God is free to flow through me into the Body of which I am part. I have said this sometimes in groups only to be met with guffaws of disbelief in such a great vocation for the human race. But if we take seriously the nature of Jesus as intercessor, brother, lamb of God, the vicarious one, how else are we to understand our selfhood, modelled after his? The gift of self is the gift of sharing in the priestliness of Christ the victim, who is our mediator because he is one of us and is wholly for us.

The priestliness of the self in the image of Christ brings us to the final aspect of our solidarity – that of the self with the earth. The Old Testament priest represented the people before God through offering to him the fruits of the earth. Inherent in this idea of priesthood is the intention of achieving unity between heaven and earth, between the created and the uncreated. This, of course, is achieved totally and eternally in the incarnate Christ. Through Christ's manhood earth finds its fulfilment in God; when he is finally all in all, then, without hindrance, the earth will be filled with the glory of God. As the Fathers of the Church and the early Cistercians saw it, Christ is the 'missing link' between God and creation and we, as creatures who also belong to heaven and to earth, similarly share this function. Through us, through our direct-edness towards God, all that he made good in the beginning may be transfused with his glory.

Such an understanding of our identity and our calling rad-ically alters our perception of the world and of our responsi-bility in it. Too often in the past Christians have wrongly identified the earth with 'the world', meaning, in effect, the dominance of ego in our social life and in our use of the goods of the earth. This has led to a denial of its destiny. An acceptance of the vanity of 'worldliness' and of the contin-gency of creation has tended to produce an attitude to creation which regards it as ultimately disposable, as a tool in God's plan, with which he will dispense at the appropriate moment. Such an approach takes no heed of our involvement with creation in our physicality: if the material world is headed for the dustbin, how can we preach the resurrection, since we, too, are material? The resurrection of Christ's body as glorified matter, matter transformed by the energy of God, has its implications for the rest of creation. To deny this is to fall foul of a kind of gnosticism which sees spirit as impris-oned in the created. Flesh and blood, our purely natural life, may not inherit the Kingdom, but in Christ that natural life is transformed by the power of the Father (1 Corinthians 15: 51–54). When St Augustine stressed that we now have a man, Jesus, interceding for us in heaven, he meant more than just a disembodied personality; he meant the total person of Jesus which involves all that he is from the earth. As Jesus is truly the son of a woman, he is truly the fruit of the earth.

There is a sense, then, in which traditional Christian theology has always been essentially 'green'. The present-day ecological crisis might well have been averted had we continued to live in this awareness of our involvement with the earth, understanding fully the consequences of our 'dominion' over nature.

Our 'lordship' over the wider creation is to be the same kind of mastery that spirit should exert over the created, material aspects of ourselves, a 'lordship' which ensures that all is directed towards God, all made available to the infusion of his Spirit. Our treatment of creation must be one which ensures its movement towards its end in God. As selves there is asked of us a respect for the natural world equal to that which we owe our bodies; a respect which acknowledges both our derivation from, and reliance upon, the earth, and our duty to give expression to its groaning for liberation. We stand before God on behalf of an otherwise mute creation just as much as we stand on behalf of one another. As Jesus told those who objected to the greetings of the disciples on his entry into Jerusalem: 'I tell you, if these keep silent the stones will cry out' (Luke 19:40).

Approaches to creation which regard it as our possession, as a disposable, renewable commodity, or which affect complete independence of it, are manifestations of ego: our current crisis is the result of a wide-scale institutionalizing of ego in the political world, in commerce, in science and technology. An adequate response to our potential ecological catastrophe must include the recovery of the full truth about our selfhood's solidarity with the earth and a willingness to live in such truth, whatever the cost. Christian involvement in ecological issues is not, then, a jumping on the bandwagon of a current fashion, a perversion of the gospel in support of political issues; such involvement is a duty, a demand issuing from our identity, an aspect of our true self-fulfilment.

This does not mean that we should all be making our banners, preparing to march on Westminster, or that we should all be building windmills in our back gardens, though for some of us it may. It does mean, for all of us, I think, an attempt to live more simply than we yet dare and a determination to resist consistently, in little ways, the exploitation of our planet. It means seeing as part of our fast from ego a fast from unnecessary consumption so that we take from the earth what is needed for our sustenance and not what is desired for the enhancement of our ego, for flight from contingency. It means accepting the whole of creation as an expression of the truths of our being. In the words of T. S. Eliot:

> They affirm Thee in living; all things affirm Thee in living; the bird in the air, both the hawk and the finch; the beast on the earth, both the wolf and the lamb; the worm in the soil and the worm in the belly. Therefore man, whom Thou hast made to be conscious of Thee, must consciously praise Thee, in thought and in word and in deed . . . Even in us the voices of seasons, the snuffle of winter, the song of spring, the drone of summer, the voices of beasts and of birds, praise Thee.

5

The self that gives itself away

'Behold, the Lamb of God . . .'

'All things affirm Thee in living.' The apparent paradox of this living in accordance with our identity as images of God is that we affirm him, too, in our dying. How totally appropriate it is that T. S. Eliot's hymn in praise of life should be part of a celebration of martyrdom. The martyr, more than any other, shows us the God who is sacrifice, who continually loses himself for those whom he has made his children and taken as his brothers and sisters. We have been looking at Jesus as our great High Priest: it is now time to consider him as the victim, 'the Lamb slain before the foundation of the world', and to explore what this means for our selfhood.

Jesus the victim does not seem to be a popular theme with us at present. Possibly this arises from our conviction that we have 'come of age' and no longer need to be 'at the mercy' of events: life is under the control of our advanced knowledge and technology. Possibly it arises, too, from our increased awareness of the bloody and painful reality so often involved in being a victim; the evidence is there, every night, on our TV screens. Possibly, for Christians and those influenced, at least, by a Christian culture, it arises also out of an approach to the cross which has presented sacrifice and suffering as ends, good in themselves, rather than as the necessary or inevitable corollaries of a way of living, a way of loving.

The sacrifice of Christ on the cross has too often been expressed to us as the demand of an implacable Justice, making the Father into a philosophical concept or a blood-thirsty and petulant tyrant, to appease whom the tender,

57

merciful Son must be immolated. Thus we make a rift in the perfect communion within the Trinity and distort understanding both of God's Fatherhood and of the nature of Christ's saving act. This view of the cross makes it a punishment, arbitrarily imposed, on an innocent victim, rather than a means of reconciliation, of atonement, in which the Father is the prime mover. This may be a bowdlerization of a theological position but it is one which holds sway in the hearts and minds of many who have rejected the God of Christianity as no more than a pagan deity demanding blood-sacrifice.

We are tempted, therefore, to highlight the resurrection in ways which diminish the reality of the cross. How often have we heard recently, even from evangelists such as Billy Graham, that the Orthodox Church emphasizes the resurrection and not the cross? To our western minds cross and resurrection are held, implicitly, in tension, in contradiction: we must stress either one or the other. The importance for us of Orthodoxy is that it does not see the tension: cross and resurrection are seen together. No Church has greater reverence for the cross because it, and it only, leads us to the resurrection.

Our other temptation is to evade the very inevitability of the cross, so that it is seen as God's making good of a human failure or as one possible response to Jesus in his surrender 'into the hands of sinful men'. In these approaches sacrifice is the result of human folly and sinfulness rather than the purpose of God.

Death and life, cross and resurrection belong together, not only in our experience or belief but also in the nature of God. The cross is God's ultimate statement of his identity and therefore of our own selfhood. Contemplation of Christ crucified and Christ risen is the surest way to self-knowledge.

The New Testament makes it abundantly clear that the sacrifice of Christ is the Father's initiative, an initiative taken out of the brooding love of God for his people which we find in the prophets Hosea and Isaiah. Christ is by nature the Lamb of sacrifice (John 1:29–30; 1 Peter 1:19–20), intended to surrender himself from all eternity (Hebrews 9:14). The will of the Father is that his Son be given up for us, a will completely embraced by the Son in the incarnation. Yet this will cannot be separated from the nature of God: what he wills, he is. God's will to give his Son expresses his self-denudation. In Jesus the denudation is also seen as an identifying characteristic of God, in the alternative translation of Philippians 2:6–7: Jesus, '*because* his state was divine, did not cling to his equality with God but *poured* himself out, to assume the condition of a slave, and become as men are'.

'To become as men are'. God in Jesus does not simply give from his store but pours himself out to become one of us, to 'become sin'. Jesus 'wastes' himself, allows himself to experience Gehenna, the rubbish-dump, the fate which human beings without God envision for themselves. If 'what he has not assumed, he has not healed' (St Gregory Nazianzen) is true, then Jesus must take into himself our humiliation, our alienation, our crushing despair and godlessness, our abandonment to the corruption of all that we have called ourselves, and in the resurrection return it to God. The great news of the cross and resurrection is that, because of God's brokenness and loss of self, nothing, absolutely nothing that we can experience is outside of God. Christ has descended into hell, into the wasteplaces, 'deeper than our sin' (Oliver Clément): here is the final healing, the final atonement. *Nothing* can separate us from the love of God. And so the cross and resurrection show us the true face of the God who wills sacrifice for his Son: the true face of the jealous God of the Old Testament, so jealous of being our only God and of our being only his that he has gone before us into hell. Christ's sacrifice shows us not a tyrant but a father 'greedy' for us, for our reconciliation with him. Only God's jealousy, God's greed, unlike our own, leads not to self-aggrandizement but to self-dispossession. In the cross we see the truth of George Mac-Donald's remark: 'If there were such a thing as a self always giving itself away, that self would be God.'

By now I am in two contradictory states: joyful at the thought of what God is and does; terrified by the consequences for my own existence and uncertain how to relate such great realities to my little, insignificant life. Fortunately the Gospels provide me with two other images of God's self-dispossession in Jesus which makes this reality of the self-as-sacrifice no less awesome but within the scope of my experience and existence. These are the images of birth and of food.

Jesus, in John's Gospel, speaks of his coming passion and death in terms of childbirth, taking up Isaiah's theme of the birth of the new, messianic age. Jesus' sacrifice is seen as the kind of loss and fulfilment occurring in pregnancy and birth. He must 'wait his time', like a woman awaiting the suffering, the passion, of labour; he must experience the 'death' of separation from the baby, of giving up what has been nurtured (which in his day might well have entailed a physical death). His last cry, 'It is accomplished', is one of self-fulfilment: Jesus has completed his labour in dying and has given birth to the 'New Man'.

This is an understanding of the relationship between sacrifice and life which we can readily appreciate and identify, however imperfectly, in our own experience, either physically or metaphorically. The pregnant woman experiences considerable loss in the time of gestation: loss of body-image and shape; loss of the body she has been accustomed to living through; loss of external activities; change in relationship with husband, friends and colleagues, owing to altered expectations and perceptions; and loss of her established status in the working-world. Loss of health, loss of life remain as real possibilities. The woman's life is truly broken, opened-up to the life of another, and permanently. When living fully she will never again be 'her old self' and will never be allowed to have a settled identity for long: children have a habit of growing, of changing, of needing us in different ways. The mother of the baby must become the mother of the newly-independent schoolchild, the rebellious teenager, the adult whose life-style, beliefs and attitudes belong to another world.

We have already seen the image of pregnancy and motherhood in connection with the self's responsibility for its growth: now we may also see it as an image of the self's manner of being in the world, as a self giving itself away.

The other great gospel image of God's daily self-dispossession is that of Jesus as food, Jesus the Bread of Life. Food is intended to be eaten, to be 'lost' in the body of the recipient, who relies on it for maintenance, for growth, for healing and repair. Jesus, in his feeding of the five thousand, and in the

Gospel of St John, shows us God as the ever-replenishing
food, forever consumed by, and lost in, his people. Jesus the
Bread of Life means strength and nourishment for us, but
vulnerability and self-dispossession for him. Jesus is the one
who is blessed by his Father, broken and distributed to the
crowd. It is, surely, significant that the disciples on the road
to Emmaus recognized Jesus in the breaking of the bread
(Luke 24:31–32). Jesus is known to them when he is experienced not only as the one with whom they had had table-
fellowship, but as the one who gives himself, like the broken
bread, for their sustenance.

What does this image of Jesus as food say about our own
selfhood? I think it is clear that we are asked to know ourselves
as food for others, as people intended to be lost for, consumed
by, others, while retaining awareness of our own sustenance
by God. The fulfilled self would find itself now consumed by
others, lost to itself in response to others: now fragmented, a
broken leftover, feeling useless, from our human viewpoint;
but, through living in acceptance of that uselessness, a powerful sign of the end-time when all will be gathered in, nothing
lost.

Understanding our selfhood as food, as bread for others,
keeps us also constantly aware both of our greatness, for on
our frail lives rests responsibility towards others, and also of
our insignificance, for we are made to be ordinary, common
bread, the daily stuff of people's existence. Our selfhood is
not generally achieved by the grand, extravagant gesture but
by the daily giving which, like bread, is so basic that it is
scarcely noticed, scarcely valued. We are called to be bread,
not caviare.

Selfhood as food also leads us, then, to a further stage in
our understanding of the place of 'denial', of sacrifice, in
Christian life. We have already seen in earlier chapters that
the self may only come to be itself in so far as it denies the
centrality of ego and renounces possession of its attributes
and existence. Now we see that the process of denial is never-
ending: the selfhood attained if ego-denial were ever completed would be the perfected image of a self-renouncing God.
Sacrifice of ego is the way to selfhood but sacrifice is also its
meaning. The repenting self, forever turning itself inside-out

61

towards God, is therefore not only denying ego but acting according to its nature; it is already beginning to reflect the image of the One to whom it is turning.

Self-fulfilment is not necessarily, then, a humanly comfortable state, for it seems to contradict all our ideas of achievement and wholeness. This vision of the self proclaims the paradoxes of the Beatitudes: when you are fragmented or used up, feeling pecked at and diminished or useless and disregarded in the effort of living towards others, then are you most truly a self, an image of the God who is poured out for us. Just as we are called to challenge the ego's belief in its being the vessel for its own existence through the act of repenting, so we are called to question the image of our selfhood as a satisfyingly whole loaf: we cannot *be* what we are made to be unless the bread is broken and given.

Our situation is like that of the 'night-girl' in George Mac-Donald's story *Photogen and Nycteris*. Kept in captivity to know only night-time and darkness as normality, her one light an alabaster globe, Nycteris experiences an open flower as damaged, distorted out of its proper shape and mercilessly exposed to the sunlight:

> I have told already how she knew the night-daisies, each a sharp-pointed little cone with a red tip; and once she had parted the rays of one of them, with trembling fingers, for she was afraid . . . perhaps she was hurting it; but she did want, she said to herself, to see what secret it carried so carefully hidden; and she found its golden heart. But now . . . stood a daisy with its red tip opened wide into a carmine ring, displaying its heart of gold on a platter of silver . . . Who could have been so cruel to the lovely little creature, as to force it open like that, and spread it heart-bare to the terrible death-lamp?
>
> But she went on thinking . . . the little Red-tip must have seen the lamp a thousand times and must know it quite well, and it had not killed it! Nay, thinking farther, she began to ask whether this might not be its more perfect condition. For not only now did the whole seem perfect . . . but every part showed its own individual perfection as well . . . The flower was a lamp itself! The golden heart

was the light and the silver border was the alabaster globe, skilfully broken and spread wide to let out the glory! Yes, the radiant shape was plainly its perfection!

God's glory has been revealed to us in the face of Christ, in the face of one broken and 'wasted' for us. God's glory is revealed in us and we find our perfection when we, too, are broken open, poured out for him and others.

This is our true, our proper state, but we know we rarely live it. To become fully ourselves asks of us a degree of lostness in God which few of us approach. Generally in our experience self and ego jostle one another for centrality in whatever we undertake. At times, circumstances evoke from us our true selves in responses which seem, from the ego's viewpoint, crazy. We take the action in an expression of essential self-hood: we live out the consequences, usually, in a messy way, with ego constantly parodying reality and obtaining gratifi-cation wherever it can. I think of the husband of a friend, who resigned from his post rather than carry out the programme of redundancies required by new management. In human terms this was an act of pure folly, an extravagant wasted gesture which could not of itself alter a system, but on God's terms, surely, an act of self-expression, of giving away one's being in solidarity with others. Now, of course, that decision taken, he is again in the world of business: the battle with ego recommences as he forges a new status; gains new satisfaction and a new self-image; strives for 'success'.

While writing about the nature of the self I have been constantly aware of the objections to this way of seeing our lives. On examination these turn out to be, in fact, objections not to true selfhood but to the ego's parodying of its character-istics. It is these parodies and other responses from ego which will occupy us now.

If I had to say whether I had ever experienced any kind of calling, any remotely realizable pressure towards one way of life, then I would have to answer that this has been how I have understood motherhood. After many years of feeling unfit, psychologically and emotionally, for child-rearing and equally many years of rejecting society's sentimentality con-cerning mothers and babies, the desire for a child seemed to emerge from a deepening awareness of spiritual pregnancy. A developing sense of spiritual 'broodiness' seemed to lead to a similar awakening at the psychological and physical levels. The discovery of infertility soon challenged this. I was convinced that, whether physical maternity was possible or not, this new responsiveness was for a purpose: I was not intended to go back to sleep on it. I had a glimpse of the meaning of selfhood.

How tempting it was, however, to make from the situation yet another image of the ego. 'Thwarted mother', 'poor victim of cruel circumstance' was an alluring image to adopt when faced with negative reactions to childlessness, real or imagined. To avoid true brokenness, how easy it is for the ego to project a picture of woundedness which attracts pity, sympathy, admiration.

Eventually I was enabled to conceive and to maintain a pregnancy and I began to see all the losses of this state as gains. Here, in motherhood, was the ordinariness, the hiddenness that had drawn me for so long. Being a postgraduate student offered no great status, but it had provided me with some kind of identity before the world and some freedom from the more humdrum aspects of 'normal' working-life. I would become one of that army of buggy-pushing mothers who 'just stay at home with the children'. No possibility of kudos there. And I would become truly available, not only to my own child but to others. That, at least, was the intention. I thought that, because I wanted all this, as well as a child of my own, so intensely and because I was persuaded of the reality of the desire by its contradiction of my temperament, it would be without rebellion, without distortion from the parodic life of my ego.

I quickly found otherwise. Poor health, and exhaustion from tending a colicky baby needing little sleep, offered scant resource against the loneliness resulting from friends' inability to accept my changed life and needs. Periods of deep depression followed. There were days of not daring to leave the house for fear of walking under a bus, days of feeling estranged from God, days of intense self-pity and hostility towards a world which could not, would not, help or even acknowledge me.

Over this time I began to see how much the true perception of the self's sacrificial nature could be distorted by the ego's desire to be a 'martyr', to be a passive recipient of gratifying sympathy; the victim-ego mocks abandonment in a spiritual lethargy which denies responsibility for co-operating with God. Passive resignation before all eventualities is accompanied by a greed for recognition of what has been, supposedly, freely offered. A thirst for the acquisition of admiration, sympathy and attention masquerades as self-renunciation. Here was I, waiting to be given, waiting to be lost, and in anguish because nobody noticed me or appreciated what I was doing! As I had recognized before, but never fully experienced, my self urged me to some kind of desert while my ego insisted on provision of a forwarding address.

Out, too, at this time went the ego-aggrandizing myth of constant availability. Availability I had seen in terms of being used by others; I had not fully appreciated that being open for others implied also knowing oneself as a humble recipient, as one made vulnerable by being continually 'on offer' and in need of response. I had forgotten that God's availability resulted in the cross. I suppose I had been persuaded by the grandiose aspirations of my ego to envision my availability as an ever-open treasure-house. I discovered, increasingly, that I was a beggar's bowl with, at times, only my emptiness to offer along with my need. And a beggar's bowl, moreover, which, all too frequently, I was intent upon keeping to myself.

So I found my ego parodying true perceptions of selfhood, reinstating the idol at the centre. More insidious, perhaps, than this mock selfhood was the ego's perseverance in clinging to its old identity, and its ingenuity in fashioning new models for itself. How easy it became to assert distinctiveness from other mothers, to hark back to past achievements or experiences in order to resist the condescension of officialdom and of the successful professionals. With what ease did the doubts take hold when friends seemed to visit only to regale me with news of their advancing projects and prospects. A zombie after three hours sleep, on such days the ego would protect itself by retreating into memory, fantasizing future achievements or aggressively asserting its denied rights and claims upon the world. When such tactics failed, the remedy remained of transforming itself into 'model mother', eschewing the life of intellect and creativity for one of dedication to its offspring. I began to see how readily one could slip from gratuitous loving of one's children into a demanding perfectionism regarding their nurture, to provide a comforting sense of attainment and success. Love, I realized, was perilously close to being seen as a boomerang: give it in order for it to return with reassurance of one's doing a superlative job.

We can never know, then, when we are truly expressing our selves for, while we may be all too aware of our mocking ego, the growing self rests hidden in God. What rests as our task is maintaining alertness to the power and resourcefulness of the 'old man's' resistance to the spirit and allowing the knowledge of our cowardice and infidelities to strip us of pretensions and illusions. We must let God have his way in the grinding process, without gathering up the dust to remould it, while letting the humiliation of our constant failure provide the power for the grindstone.

My continuing experience of beginning to live with my nose rubbed, as it were, in the dust of the 'old man', the ego, has made me understand spiritual life in an entirely new way, as a journey deep into Godlessness rather than out of it. Increasingly I see that it is in going deeper into the derelict places within us, where we curse and deny God, in resting without flinching in the knowledge of our distance from God, that we encounter Christ waiting for us in the depth of hell. I am beginning to grasp just why that great Orthodox monk, Staretz Silouan, heard those words from Christ: 'Keep thy mind in hell and despair not.' When we allow grief at the reality of our own and humanity's estrangement from God to grind and consume us, while looking to Christ the Lamb and Harrower of Hell, do we not glimpse in our own lives the vision attained by the martyr, St Ignatius of Antioch: 'I am God's wheat, and I am ground by the teeth of wild beasts, that I may be found pure bread of Christ'?

6

Narcissus at prayer? – the self and modern spirituality

'For you have died and your life is hidden with Christ in God'
(Colossians 3:3)

Anyone who has persevered so far in reading this book will have realized that the understanding of selfhood it presents calls into question not only our popular understanding of the person but also some of our modern guiding notions about Christian formation and spirituality which are based upon it. In this chapter I want to establish from this vision of self a base for evaluating and using some of the concepts and methods current in modern formation and spiritual direction.

Contemporary formation in Christian life leans heavily upon the idea of the 'faith-story' of the individual, upon sharing one's own experience of the search for God (or, more often, God's search for us). In principle this is extremely useful. It helps to root what may seem to be high-flown, abstract ideas in the realities of ordinary life; it bridges the gap between doctrine and the messy, muddled business of living. It helps us to appreciate that God does, indeed, touch our lives and ask for intimacy with us. It brings home to us the constancy of God's love amidst all our infidelity and tepidity and our potential for response to him.

The great danger, however, with this approach is that all too often it remains 'my story', the account of an individual, to which others are invited to respond as individuals. If we are not careful we then 'sell' religion as we sell soap – 'this experience can be yours, too' – as an appeal to the individual to make another acquisition or to better himself or herself.

Rarely is the personal story firmly established as that of a person, a being who tells, for all of us, his or her particularized version of the love-story of God and the human race. As a result, the Christian Church is then envisaged as a collection of individuals sharing similar experiences and similar beliefs rather than as a community of persons participating in the same identity, the same vocation, the same destiny.

Emphasis on faith-story may also, rather than bridging the gap, drive a wedge between experience and doctrine. When the focus is 'my experience' it is frighteningly easy, when there is no safeguarding concept of the self, to appropriate that experience to the ego, to see it as a truth uniquely 'my' possession. 'What I experience' may then become the norm by which I judge biblical and church teaching. 'That is not my experience, therefore that is no longer valid' is the response frequently offered individually and collectively where the telling of one's story is central to formation. We no longer say 'I believe in order to understand' but 'I have not come to an experiential understanding of this, therefore it is not worth believing'. We quickly set what is within our compass, and, generally, what gratifies our ego, as our limit.

When we are led to set our own 'faith-story' within the concept of selfhood, how different is the outcome. We learn to set our particular experience within the context of God's story of his relationship with, and purposes for, humankind. We allow that experience to be judged, to be sifted, by the wider community of the Church, known in the Bible and in Christian history. Thus, what speaks genuinely of God, echoing in our time and in a little way that accumulated Christian knowledge of his ways, may more readily be discerned and validated; what is of our ego, a product of our idiosyncrasies and temperament, may be allowed to fade. Then our personal faith-stories take their place in the general current of the Christian story, valuable because of what they say about God and not because they are ours.

In the same way that the 'personal story' appears to dominate our approach to Christian formation so the dictum 'holiness equals wholeness' seems still to be central to our modern spirituality. 'Wholeness', in this context, generally applies to psychological and emotional well-being and maturity, to the eradication of our personality disorders, to the healing-over of our psychological wounds. In such an approach 'humanity' is totally identified with psycho-physical being, with ego. Since Jesus is perfectly human it follows quite naturally, according to this view, that psychological perfection, that is, completeness or wholeness, should be seen as the goal of Christian life, as our way of becoming images of Christ. The intention is wholly admirable, to understand our holiness as the reflection of the holiness of God incarnate; the result is a shift of focus from God to individuals and their development, an equation of the quest for psychological maturity with the quest for God.

As we have seen in earlier chapters the wholeness which is holiness for the Christian is not integrity *within* the personality but the integration of body and soul, our 'carnal' man, with spirit and thence with God. Such wholeness therefore denotes not completeness, absence or brokenness or flaws, but *single-ness*, an overcoming of internal dividedness. The early Fathers of the desert were called monks, 'monachos', meaning single, not because they lived alone but because they sought a state of interior unification in which the entire person is unified as body-soul-spirit in directedness towards God. Wholeness therefore implies simplicity, a state of unity, of oneness, reflecting divine simplicity, in distinction from our complexity, our state of combat between body-soul and spirit with all the inner fragmentation and dissipation of energy arising from it. To be whole is to have unified all our desires into the one, simple desire for God; it is to be *wholly* intent, with the *whole* of our powers, upon God, single-minded, single-hearted, single-willed in the pursuit of total responsiveness to God. Wholeness in this sense is the state of union with God, in which the division between God and humankind is finally dissolved: something which we pursue but God alone gives. It can be summed up for us by the prayer of that saint who could never be claimed as the model of psychological perfection, St Francis of Assisi: 'My God and my all'.

When applied to the self, therefore, wholeness means both more and less than when applied to the ego. More, because it refers to a radical unification at the heart of a person, to a healing at the roots of his or her sinful, divided state. Here wholeness must mean holiness, for it is truly the perfecting of our selves as images of Christ. 'Wholeness is union', yes, indeed.

Such spiritually-based wholeness means less than its psychological counterpart in that it implies the attainment neither of completeness nor of flawlessness within the personality. As we have seen, brokenness is an essential aspect of our lives, our means of becoming like God in the experience both of ego-denial and self-fulfilment. As selves we are essentially unwhole, open-ended, looking to Another for our completeness. As selves, too, we are bound in with our brothers and sisters and our world; we cannot, therefore, speak of a wholeness which has no reference to the consummation of all things in Christ. We dare not establish any understanding of human wholeness which denies that terrible reality of the tension between 'the already and the not yet'.

The conscious, direct pursuit of psychological wholeness may lead us away from the real need of seeking singleness of intention upon God, just as the determined quest for physical fitness may result in physical and psychological loss of well-being. Identifying physical fitness as our main goal may lead to the overdevelopment of muscle tissue and the stress injuries which make our bodies less, rather than more, healthy, while excessive concentration upon such 'fitness' narrows the range of our interests and our freedom in relationships. We live through, and not for, our bodies.

The determination to achieve psychological maturity may similarly lead us to feeling the necessity for a constant psychological fitness programme, an agenda of the 'hang-ups' and weaknesses to be probed and resolved. Rather than becoming freer to respond to others, we grow increasingly concerned with our own reactions in any situation. Out of our habit of interpreting every word and action we lose the ability to accept the need for playfulness in human relationships (except, of course, when we have decided that play is essential to wholeness!). Our true psychological wholeness is, in fact, reduced, because we have narrowed our interest to our psyche alone, neglecting the reality of the world around us and our response to it. Spiritually we have slid into idolatry, into

making a contingent means of being in the world, our personalities, into self-sufficient ends.

The need for psychological healing and development, then,
must be clearly distinguished from the growth to maturity of
the self, which is realization of the image of Christ within us
(Ephesians 4:14–16). Once this has been achieved we are
then able to say, as I have already suggested, 'I am through
my personality', just as we may already say, 'I am through
my body'. If I break my leg I seek medical help but do not
feel diminished as a person. If I become depressed I equally
obtain medical care but do not, again, consider my selfhood
reduced by the experience. Only sin, the choice of ego in
opposition to God, can do this. If my leg then requires ampu-
tation I grieve, I acknowledge the pain and the anger involved
in the loss. Whatever opportunities arise to improve my situation, such as an improved prosthesis, I take, but my life and
relationships will not be governed by incessant searching for
'the answer' to my physical disability; I live through my body,
in its new state, just as I lived through it in its previous
condition. My experiences, my activities may be vastly altered
but my selfhood suffers no diminution. Similarly, if I discover
that behind my reactive depression is a depressive personality,
I take whatever openings there are for learning new ways of
coping with expectations, with guilt, with the gap between
inner and outer reality, while acknowledging the limits of the
undertaking as being, as Freud once said, 'the conversion of
my hysterical misery into normal unhappiness'. I recognize
that my self lives through all that happens to my psyche, that
the purpose in therapy is not the perfecting of personality but
the liberating of my ego from some of the false beliefs which
inhibit its response to spirit. Rather than developing from
this a permanent 'agenda', a programme of continuing ego-
development, I will see this time of conscious examination of
my ego as limited, as a season which must die if another
season of growth is to follow. I will then be free to live
through, rather than as, my personality, frequently suffering
it but acknowledging it as the bit of creation I am asked to
reconcile with God.

I encountered this equation of wholeness with holiness
during the early part of social-work training, when my 'prob-

lem in using authority' was identified. My extreme diffidence made it agonizingly difficult for me to perform social-work tasks which required the exercise of any kind of legal power and authority. It was, and still is, a real wound. I was really quite useless with those who needed confrontation with the harsh game of consequences which governs much of our life in society: if you do not pay gas bills, the gas supply is disconnected. I knew I was useless and it hurt. I knew also, although dimly, that for some people my wound offered a way into themselves. My inability to assume any right to be in their homes and in their lives appeared to them like a tacit affirmation of their rights, of their value, so that they felt safe to let down defences and risk admission of failure themselves. For them it was my weakness which enabled them to be strong enough to admit theirs, my lack of psychological wholeness that made me a safe place in which to examine their wounds.

At this time I could not articulate what I vaguely felt and I labelled the phenomenon as strictly a problem, as a lack of wholeness. I grew increasingly anxious, and depressed about the anxiety. My lack of wholeness was all too apparent; if wholeness was equivalent to holiness, and holiness was 'full humanity', conceived psychologically, then was I not inadequately human? To be human evidently rested in the possession of the right number and right kind of personality attributes – all those I quite clearly lacked! The seeds were sown for the depressive illness which was to follow and the nub of my spiritual problem was revealed, could I but have seen it. At the same time anxiety about this situation turned attention away from clients' needs onto my own. Instead of being for them, making me more fully a self, I was caught up in monitoring my own responses. So I fell simultaneously into two traps: into equating ego with spirit, psychological weakness with spiritual dis-ease, with sin; into turning the expression of selfhood into an act to be evaluated and possessed by the ego.

'Holiness is wholeness' may lead others, as it did me, down the path of psychological perfectionism. It may also further belief in the equation of holiness with the possession of psychological gifts. Our concept of wholeness may include

72

not only the absence of 'hang-ups' but also the presence of a balanced development of personality attributes, which gives rise to the rounded, 'whole' person. I recall the heady days of the French 'events of May' in 1968 when this 'whole man' was being advocated, a person, who, to be fully human, must be at once sportsman, philosopher, craftsman and clown. A noble vision in some ways, but one which equates manhood with the possession and development of psycho-physical attributes. A vision, too, shared today by many leaders in our churches, for how often do we find urged upon us, from an exposition of the parable of the talents, the development of all our gifts as our means of entry into the Kingdom? We are so possessed by the notion that selfhood equals personality that we can only read this parable as speaking of literal talents, of gifts of a physical or psychological nature. Surely this parable really refers, not to such ephemeral gifts, but to the great gift of spirit, of capacity for responsiveness to God, which we foster or stifle? When we have grasped that God has, indeed, given us the greatest gift of all, a share in his life through Christ, do we not then see that the development of lesser gifts, however desirable in itself, must at all times be subservient to the maintenance and nurture of that life? We are called to live as gifts, with Jesus, to the Father. This is the true source of balance, of fullness, in our lives.

If 'wholeness' needs to be assessed in the light of our knowledge of selfhood, equally in need of evaluation are those two other key images in modern spirituality: growth and the journey.

Growth in selfhood, earlier chapters have suggested, contradicts our commonsense notions about becoming bigger and acquiring further improved assets. The growing self experiences, by contrast, an increasing awareness of poverty, an increasing ability to rejoice in its nothingness and in its absolute dependence upon God. Like St John the Baptist, its motto is 'He must increase, I must decrease' (John 3:30–31).

This does not mean that our personalities must, of necessity, shrink or remain undeveloped; far from it. It does imply, however, that such development will not be our central concern and goal. If our hearts are set upon the Kingdom of God, his transforming rule over us, all else that *he* judges

73

needful will be given us (cf. Matthew 6:33). If we understand
by growth the unfolding of the seed of the Kingdom within
us, we will be freed from that anxiety about our stature which
is incapable of affecting our size (Matthew 6:27).

The kind of growth we must seek, then, is growth in self-
forgetfulness. This is, in itself, almost a contradiction in terms
for we cannot achieve such forgetfulness by remembering to
practise it! It can only be left to develop unawares, as a
natural consequence of our preoccupation with God. When
we look to God, he looks after us. The only way to true
growth, then, is to surrender ourselves to God the 'good
gardener', assisting him by weeding our soil through fasting
from ego.

If we wish to learn what spiritual growth might mean for
us we can do no better than listen to the teaching of those
masters of spiritual abandonment, St Francis de Sales and
Jean-Pierre de Caussade, both champions of the ideal of holiness for all.

The consistent theme of St Francis' direction is the hiddenness of ourselves in God and the folly of our persistent anxiety
about our spiritual dimensions. Francis combined teaching
upon the person's proper responsibility for cultivation of 'the
little virtues' of humility, gentleness and meekness (all characteristic of Jesus' humanity) with an emphasis upon the primacy of God's activity in our growth. Thus he advised
Madame Brulart, one of his spiritual 'children', in her desire
to direct her own development: 'Trees only bear fruit in the
presence of the sun. Let us dwell in the presence of God which
will help us, sooner or later, to bear fruit.'

Feverish worry about our own growth was, for Francis, a
sign of domination by ego, of love of ego supplanting love of
God. True development occurs when the person wants only
what God wants, when he wants it and in the way he wants
it: all else is the ego's desire to be in control at the centre and
to see emerging a satisfying image of a 'spiritual person'.
For Francis an indication of growth in true selfhood is the
acceptance of our present state of life as the way to holiness
for us. Too many of us, he saw, dream of attaining a type of
holiness impossible in the here and now, because it appeals
to our ego. Like a flower, to grow we must accept the kind

of flower we are and the nature of the soil nurturing our roots, so that we 'bloom where we are planted'.

Another indication of growth, in Francis' spirituality, is readiness to accept being hidden from one's own scrutiny and indifference to the pleasure or pain endured in looking to God. The absence of a reflectiveness upon our feelings and states of mind which diverts our attention from God is a sure sign of spiritual health:

> What difference does it make whether you are on Thabor or on Calvary, in this state or in that? Happy is the soul that seeks God alone, for she will find everywhere what she seeks, and she will seek everywhere what she has. He who loves the Divine Master alone serves him cheerfully and with great equality at all times, without considering whether the effects will be useful, profitable or hurtful.

The self must learn to accept growing, blooming and declining, rain and drought, so as to become, as it were, a beautiful flower for God, if only, in its own eyes, an unsightly weed.

For Jean-Pierre de Caussade growth similarly meant self-abandonment to God through the external circumstances and the inner promptings of daily life. The growing self is one which is indifferent to whether it appears to be developing or not, which has abandoned all concern for itself to God, happy in the frailty that makes it more fully a simple, poor, capacity for God:

> Let us hide behind (the flawed life of our personality) and rejoice in God who is our only good. Let us make use of our frailty, hardships, these cares, this need for food and clothing and possessions, these failures, suspicion of others, these doubts and anxieties, these perplexities, and find our joy in God who, through them, gives himself wholly to us to be our only blessing . . .
>
> God wants to be the source of everything in us that is holy, and for that reason everything that depends on ourselves and on our personal faith is insignificant and quite the opposite of saintliness.
>
> We can never achieve anything great except through surrendering ourselves; therefore let us think no more about

it. Let us leave the care of our salvation to God. He knows the way . . . Let us march on in the trivial duties of our personal devotion without aspiring to great ones . . . let us be content to love him unceasingly and walk humbly in the path he has marked out for us, where all seems so trivial in our own eyes and in the eyes of the world.

To grow is nothing more than to increase our receptivity to God. And in such development, in which we seem to lose so much, our true distinctiveness is being preserved and enhanced by God:

All of us partake of divine life; although Jesus Christ is different in each one, he himself remains the same. The life of each individual is the life of Jesus, a new testament. The face of the Lord is a border of sweetly smelling flowers. Divine action is the gardener who arranged the plants so expertly that the border is unlike any other. Among all the flowers there is not one alike, except in their common surrender to the hand of the gardener, leaving him complete mastery over them, to do what he likes, content for their part to do what is their nature and state to do.

For St Francis and for de Caussade true growth is growth in God-centredness. In our modern spirituality, growth is all too often located within the ego, for the ego. Increasingly we are urged to join courses and retreats concerned with 'personal growth', focusing us not beyond ourselves on God but on our egos and their enhancement. Rather than promoting the radical self-forgetfulness found in St Francis and de Caussade they encourage concern with our own abilities, efforts and needs which establishes our personalities as our centre.

This danger within contemporary spirituality is exemplified for me in an advertising trailer for a recent book on eucharistic adoration. To many readers this may be a practice neither congenial nor theologically acceptable. I ask them simply to take this illustration as an example and to accept that for those who do engage in it, it is adoration of Jesus with us as the Bread of Life, Christ with us in the power of his Easter sacrifice and victory, and in the hiddenness and humility of his incarnation. Such adoration calls us beyond concern with ego, so that we become 'lost' in the mystery of God incarnate and transcendent. To the advertisers, however, Christians are to be encouraged to try this form of prayer by the question: 'Have you been neglecting this valuable tool for your spiritual growth?' Priorities here are entirely reversed. No longer is God the Mystery before whom we prostrate ourselves in self-forgetfulness but our means to a bigger, supposedly more 'spiritual', ego. Prayer is no more a means of growing in relationship with God, allowing ourselves to be lost through transformation into him, but a 'tool' with which to make an improved 'self'-image. The cult and cultivation of ego has replaced surrender to the hand of God the cultivator.

A similar shift in focus can be seen in our present use of the image of the journey. As an image for the process of the life of faith we need to take that fundamental journey of the Israelites out of Egypt. This journey is corporate, initiated by God; its purpose is the fulfilment of God's design for his people. It is not a journey undertaken for the sake of the ego-development of individual Israelites; its end is the establishment of a people of God. The attention of the travellers must be directed not upon their own experiences, their own plans and desires, but upon the God who leads them. When this attention falters, when the journey is appropriated to themselves in preoccupation with their losses, their needs, their ideas of what is necessary and appropriate for them, disorder and idolatry ensue.

In the New Testament the journey which could be regarded as paradigmatic for us is that of the prodigal son back to his Father's house, the return of alienated Man to his source in God, recapitulated for us in the death of Christ. The journey is thus one out of 'the land of unlikeness' to God, to the place of union, to restoration as a 'first-born son', an image of *the* First-Born. This journey is an image of conversion, of increasing conformity to Christ, involving the experience of loss and brokenness we see in the Israelites, in the Prodigal, in Jesus.

Such an image, then, needs to be used personally, not individually, to speak not of our psychological experience along the way but of our particularized undergoing of *the* journey of humankind to God, as an illustration of God's dealings with us. The image should take us beyond our egos towards contemplation of God and humanity. So it does in its traditional use in spiritual writings, nowhere better, perhaps, than in Walter Hilton's *The Scale of Perfection*.

Hilton uses the idea of the pilgrimage to Jerusalem as a metaphor for the process of conversion and transformation into a perfect image of Christ. Although he discusses the problems and obstacles on the journey, his desire is to focus his reader not on any individual way of experiencing these difficulties but upon the destination: Jesus. Psychological and spiritual barriers must be considered, but only within the context of advancing the journey. Self-forgetful looking to Jesus is all that is truly necessary, as Hilton makes clear in discussing the initial urge to make a pilgrimage:

> If you wish to learn the nature of this desire, it is, in fact, Jesus himself. He implants this desire within you, and is himself the desire and the object of your desire. If you could only understand this, you would see that Jesus is everything and Jesus does everything.

Happenings on the way are consequently important only in so far as they illuminate or obscure this reality. The traveller is not to be concerned with accumulating riches of any kind, whether they be a sure knowledge of the way, a 'satisfactory' prayer-life, or an acceptable picture of oneself as a pilgrim. The pilgrims' one resource for the way, against all eventualities, must be knowledge of their nothingness and the all-sufficiency of God, so that each can say only and always: 'I am nothing, I have nothing, I desire nothing but the love of Jesus.'

Hilton was writing in the fourteenth century, from an accumulation of Christian wisdom and experience of the conflict between self and ego, 'old man' and 'new man'. Our present-day popular use of the image would appear, in many instances, to represent a radical break with this understanding both of the image of the journey and the understanding of the Christian task. In attempting, rightly, to assert the necessity of a personal response to God, but believing that personality constitutes our 'person', our self, we have come to understand the journey wholly in terms of the experiences of the ego. We no longer consider 'the Christian journey' but '*my* journey in faith' or, very often, 'my journey of self-discovery'. We are increasingly invited to undertake a pilgrimage not to God in himself but to a state of self-awareness assumed to involve an awareness of God. We need to recover the distinction made by the great Christian mystics between seeking God in ourselves and seeking ourselves in God. In the first instance, we desire God. Knowing that he dwells hidden within us we 'journey inwards' for *his* sake, to find him, to be for him. That this journey is into ourselves and may result in self-knowledge is entirely incidental and of no importance. If God were not within, we would not embark upon the journey. In the second case, we are dissatisfied and unsure of ourselves; the ego then seeks in God awareness of its identity and the enhancement of its image and status. How easy it is to believe we are looking for God through prayer, through a disciplined spiritual life, only to find that we have slipped into desiring greater maturity, the idea of ourselves as 'spiritual', the vision of ourselves as 'people on the way'. We have put God to work for our egos.

Consciousness of this tendency towards idolatry of ego in modern spirituality, arising from our confusion over concepts and images, should lead us also to caution in our approach to those systems currently influential in retreat-leading and spiritual direction: Myers-Briggs typology and the Enneagram.

The Myers-Briggs typology is a development of Carl Jung's analysis of personality into four basic types. Myers-Briggs proposes eight different personality-types; discernment of our individual type is said to lead to greater self-knowledge and freedom to accept 'what we are' (understood in our terms as our ego). Such awareness of our type is also held to be an indicator of the appropriate kind and method of prayer for each of us, liberating us from fruitless attempts to follow other ways. The freedom and knowledge thus gained is, of course, entirely confined to our personality, our ego; as we have seen, the hidden, dynamic self is not available to such analysis and categorization.

Within these limits such a system may be helpful in loosening the restrictions upon our personality and increasing docility to the spirit. On the other hand, the certainty with which its practitioners appear to handle their categories would seem also to limit freedom to respond to the Holy Spirit who so frequently leads us to ways of praying and acting which transcend our personalities. Furthermore, such certainty that this is the way to discover our selfhood binds us firmly to our egos, however expanded and enlightened they may now be. We are, essentially, caught up in looking, skilfully, for the living among the dead.

In this way both Man and God are reduced. Man is summed up by his personality and Jesus, the God-Man, is regarded in his manhood solely as a model for our personality. As some of the practitioners of the systems maintain, since Jesus is perfect man, perfect personality, we *must* be able to find all eight character-types within him, in their perfection. Personhood is thus supplanted by personality; Jesus, Saviour and Brother, Jesus the restorer of all things to God, becomes Jesus model for one's personality. Our creation as the image and likeness of God, as sons and daughters in the Son, as brothers and sisters in the Brother, our identity as priest and lamb of sacrifice are here overlooked; in its place we have a superficial vision of likeness to Christ in the sharing of personality attributes. Surely this is a petty Christianity which can say little to a world struggling with the realities of the consequences from our love-affair with egotism. Proclamation of a God who is limited to the bounds of these same egos is scarcely the 'Good News' with which the Churches can advance into the decade of evangelization. A secularized world needs more than a secularized, personality-centred faith.

Understood as a tool of limited scope Myers-Briggs typology has its uses: as an approach to spirituality it is dangerous in its effects upon our vision of human personhood. As much may be said also of that other popular system, the Enneagram, a personality typology derived from Sufi mysticism.

The Enneagram presupposes an innocent 'self' which becomes distorted and fixated as a result of social pressures into one of nine compulsive survival-strategies; in its terminology, the ego. Growth is a matter of 'redeeming' the compulsion in order to bring about a free 'surrendering to our essence' and a subsequent discovery of selfhood.

Superficially similar in terminology to our Christian concept of selfhood, this system is fundamentally at variance with it, for it operates totally within the personality. The 'self' is not a capacity for God, a receptiveness of spirit to Spirit, which leaves us locating our source beyond ourselves. Rather, it is conceived of as 'the focus of one's inner resources and strength'. We are talking of the unknown potential of the ego, of our personality regarded as its own possession. As a result, when the 'ego' is 'redeemed' from its compulsions it surrenders, not to a Being beyond itself, but to its own 'essence', to that fuller, hitherto unrealized, personality. Approached simply as a means of untying the knots in our personalities this system may prove of value. However, that it is understood and taught as a way to liberating the self makes it potentially perilous: freed only to know more about our egos, we believe we have realized ourselves. Instead of losing ourselves to be found in the infinity of God, we are actually binding ourselves to the limits of our psycho-physical nature. We have substituted, in this system, realization of ego for realization of our essentially self-transcending nature.

As Christians we have been caught in the proverbial pendulum swing: reacting against a form of spirituality which emphasized depravity in the individual and detachment from others, to an almost Manichaean extent, we are now enmeshed in an idolatry of all things human. Our pressing need is not to establish a balance between these two positions, but to recover our vision of Man as 'The Golden Dustman', as Charles Dickens named him. Man the Golden Dustman derives all his treasures from the dustiness of his earthiness, his humanity, but only when he has allowed this dust to be transformed in his surrendering to the process of death and resurrection. Our humanity is our wealth only when it is no longer ours, but God's; our modern spirituality will only deserve its name when it can lead us to surrender our humanity to God so that, in the words of Blessed Elizabeth of the Trinity, we may become 'another incarnation, in which God may renew all his mysteries'.

7

The self in the Body of Christ – selfhood and community

'You are to be blessed, broken and distributed, that the work of the incarnation may go forward' (St Augustine)

'I am because you, God, are' is, we have seen, the self's basic statement of its identity. To be a person is to accept living in and through the spiritual relationships of 'childship' and 'brotherhood', and living them to the full. We cannot make a unilateral declaration of independence from God and from others without distorting and denying ourselves. We similarly reject our status as persons wherever we refuse our differentiation from God and others, wherever we attempt to claim identity with God by nature rather than as gift or to merge our particularity into the mass, the collective. Just as the persons of the Blessed Trinity are distinctive, yet wholly God and truly a unity, so we, as persons, sum up humankind without losing our uniqueness. Hence it was possible for St Paul to speak of each Christian growing to the full stature of Christ (Ephesians 4:13) and of our composing the one Body of Christ. As members of that Body we are each our own special image of Christ, playing our part, uniquely, in the whole. Together we form a complex, highly differentiated, interdependent organism, not a 'glob' in which each cell is unable to be distinguished from any other.

When we view ourselves in this light the apparent opposition between the private or individual and the communal resolves itself as an irrelevance. We begin to see that if we are, indeed, sons, daughters, brothers, sisters, intercessors, then any experience of solitude, of our inner desert, is not for ourselves alone. Our search for God is shifting the focus for all of us, it has a worldwide significance. So, what may feel like 'a flight of the alone to the Alone' brings us to a heaven which is *peopled*, to the City of God. We often talk too easily about finding God in other people, forgetting that the converse is also true. Abba Dorotheus, one of the great Fathers of the desert, once described our journey to God as being along the spokes of a wheel: the closer to God, the closer to one another; only in him do we all fully meet. Once grasped, this vision of our communion as persons gives us a new way of looking at the individual–community tension in our liturgy and worship. It enables us also to articulate a response to social and political issues which proceeds directly from our doctrine of Man.

Our present state of mind with regard to worship is extremely easy to caricature. On the one hand is the person who goes to church solely for communication with God and thus resents the 'unnecessary intrusion' of others. Liturgy is the opportunity for a heart-to-heart with the Lord in which the mere presence of others is tolerable. Dominant here is an individualism which makes of bonding an optional extra. On the other hand is the liturgical enthusiast who insists that such prayer is to be in common so that our personal response is secondary to a collective expression of faith. Here the 'Body' is in danger of being envisaged as an undifferentiated 'glob' in which all parts exercise the same function simultaneously. The particularity of the person is here lost in the whole.

If we consider our worship as that of a Body of persons, with their own distinctive call to be a particular image of Christ, I think we can evolve a new approach. The essential sign of the Church as the Body can now be seen in the coming together, the being together, in a common consent to focus all on the Lord; in the case of liturgical worship a common consent to the central actions which constitute it. Active, corporate participation is then not identified simplistically with everyone doing and saying everything together but rather with the common action of concentrating everything upon the Lord through the words and movements of our worship. It means that as a Body we are unifying ourselves in body, mind and spirit in attentiveness to God: as the popular song says: 'Let's forget about ourselves, and concentrate on him and worship him.' For some this may well demand a response of silence, letting the words and actions be and saying 'yes' to them, in apparent inattentiveness to the people around. Understood in this way, such a response is not selfishly individualistic but a reaching down to the core where we meet and know communion in God. For others, this attentiveness may only be achieved by the fullest possible physical engagement in all the actions and words of our worship. For many there will be a personal balance between these two, changing according to the differing phases of their relationship with God. In the Catholic Church the present Pope has made it clear that the nature of liturgical participation may differ according to the nature of the particular religious order concerned: a community of hermits such as the Carthusians will interpret 'participation' in a way which reflects their calling to silence and solitude. What is true of religious families within one Church is, I believe, true of any family of Christian worshippers. Liturgical worship, worship in common should not require the person to abandon the way to which God has called him or her but to live it to its fullness in a common sharing with brothers and sisters in Christ. To return to de Caussade's image of the face of the Lord as a border of flowers, when the Church gathers as Christ's Body his beauty and his features are better delineated by the differences in colour and shape which compose the whole than by a uniformity.

This must not be read as an invitation to anarchy, as it would indeed be, when interpreted from an individualist viewpoint. The self, recognizing its responsibility to and for the life of the Body, does not 'do its own thing' in sublime disregard for others. It must embrace the demand for constant discernment of motive so that the response to the Lord's call to silence, to dancing, to praying through our bodies does not become our chosen way of expressing our imagined distinctness from the community. There may, indeed, be times when we must endure the very real pain of resisting response when it would distract or distress others. Although none of us may feel we need fear the same experience we can, perhaps, learn from the life of St Teresa of Avila who had frequently to fight the ecstasies which drew too much attention from her nuns.

What this means for us, in practical terms, is that we need to rethink our attitude to silence and to consider the place in common worship of corporate recollection, receptivity, and fasting from ego as the corollary of corporate expression.

Popular thinking is dominated by a rather facile distinction: silence implies individuality while speech or song implies togetherness. How often in a service, after a period of common prayer, are we invited to a time of silence for 'our own' petitions. After a period of communion we are then seen to retreat into 'our' concerns, as though the common prayer was in an entirely distinct category. Silence is assumed to divide rather than unite. A moment's thought will reveal the fallacy. How often, in public prayer, have you found yourself ending the Lord's Prayer before you have even realized you had begun it? I know I have. It is all too easy to default in spirit from the activity of the Body while physically engaged upon it. Similarly, how often do we find that we are using words not to communicate, that is, to establish communion, but to build a wall around ourselves, so that we can defend ourselves and refuse relationship while appearing to maintain it? Silence may equally be a stone wall, a retreat into ego, but it may also be a return to the centre where we meet others in God, a concentration upon spirit in which we recognize our true identity. I first started to write this after the disaster at the Hillsborough football stadium in 1989. Here in Nottingham we have just had a three-minutes silence in the city centre for all the dead. People here felt a great need simply to be together, expressing powerfully in their common silence the loss, the incomprehension, the pain that was theirs. They discovered a bond in their grief more adequately expressed by their silent attentiveness to the dead than by any number of words. It has frequently been said in this catastrophe that football has quasi-religious status in Britain: may it not be that the opportunity here afforded to express a deeper reciprocity, a belonging to one another in vulnerability and play, through silence and symbol (the flowers, the football scarves) meets a need left unsatisfied by our over-rational, word-dominated modern liturgies?

As persons we are 'capacities for God'; our liturgies therefore, to be true to our nature, must similarly make of our
communities 'spaces' for God. True worship must have
silence, in which we can enter our 'hearts' and attend to God;
it must have spaciousness, in which there is room to receive
and absorb what is given. Then spoken 'responses' may be
truly responses, emerging from what has been taken and
dwelt upon. If the silence and space threaten and discomfort
us, then God is, indeed, speaking to his people of their dis-
ease, of their fear of exposure to his presence.

Liturgy such as this is fundamentally turned outwards
towards God, expressive of our nature rather than of our
wonderful ideas and thoughts about him. We are maintained
in our identity as people made to receive their being from
God and to return it to him in thanksgiving. It therefore
celebrates our poverty and his transcendence as the true way
to affirming his indwelling: we leave space from our words
for him, the Word, 'to dwell among us'. Our egos, however,
look for escape from this awareness of receptivity, into more
satisfying activity, which stresses human importance. In this
situation the highlighting of God's immanence becomes a
flight from acceptance of poverty. It is more gratifying to fill
the spaces with enjoyable words or music which testify to
personal skills and insights than to wait in a humble, if
uncomfortable, silence upon the Lord. Thus we can so often
distort the Eucharist, for example, by letting the sharing of
the kiss of peace become an extended expression of individual
feelings. This sharing of our warmth for others may appear
more like the love of God than the directing of our will
towards him in forgetfulness of our special fondness for X and
our unease with Y. And so the peace, far from establishing our
identity as brothers and sisters in Christ in a peace annihilat-
ing our individual attractions and repugnances, serves to
enhance our individualism by emphasizing our regard for
differing personalities. Yes, 'the peace' should communicate
acceptance and warmth: acceptance of our neighbour as 'the
Temple of the Shekinah', the dwelling-place of God, and our
brother; warmth from the fire of God's love which burns,
however feebly, within us. Furthermore, this 'peace' should
be, not an end in itself, but a preparation for the time of full

oneness in Holy Communion, when we are most completely personal, united with others because united with God.

Eschewing this temptation to become a community celebrating personality requires us to engage in a corporate fast from ego. This may be helped by the use of familiar texts in worship, in two, apparently contradictory, ways. The familiar may invite contempt or the automatic response but to engage our wills in complete attention to its content allows no room for ego-seeking novelty. It calls us to go deeper, beneath the surface of the text, in a way rarely possible when we experience constant change in order, in translation of texts, in wording. We have to exert ourselves to remain alert to what God is saying to us, how he is teaching us to find him in all that we have taken for granted.

The familiar may also, as we have seen in earlier chapters, have provided us with God-directed mental furnishing. Acquaintance with wording enables us to concentrate, not on surface detail, but on the deeper significances of a text: we are not diverted by the change in nuance, or meaning itself, from the central thrust of prayer or reading. Familiarity with the content and shape of a liturgy helps us quickly to know our place, spiritually, within the worship, to get 'into the groove' of its Godward movement. The well-known words, phrases, images reverberate within us, evoking our slowly-developed, abiding response to God and leaving our ego with less room to cast about for diversion.

To many people, I am sure, this will seem to be advocating a return to a barren formalism in which week after week we repeat the same exterior process which neither engages us personally nor expresses our hopes and our needs. A formalism which excludes the human from worship: don't worry about your fainting neighbour, you're here to praise God. It is very easy indeed for an approach to liturgy which asks for awareness of God's transcendence and fasting from ego to decline into parody. Yet is this not the truth about all our endeavour, a truth which, far from removing the need to attempt the ideal, makes it all the more important that we strive to approach it? The lasting tension in our worship is not, in truth, that between the collective and the individual, as we have seen. It is between maintaining and expressing the reality of the God-who-is-with-us as also the God-who-is-beyond-us. To sustain this requires a constant fast from ego and the constant vigilance which must always be its companion.

We have been made painfully aware in recent years of the loneliness experienced by many Christians and searchers, as a result of the individualism or overdeveloped group identity found in our churches. All too true, sadly, is the story of the newcomer who steadfastly wore his hat through a number of Sunday services. When finally approached about his gaffe, he explained, with some relief, that it was the only way to ensure contact! Creating a welcoming community has become, in reaction to this kind of situation, a priority for many congregations, a priority made even more important by awareness of the breakdown of relationship experienced in our social world.

This grasp of the primacy of community is long overdue and much to be valued. Our present approach to it, however, presents problems in so far as we have come to understand ourselves as obliged to *create* community. We tend to assume that we are individuals needing to be moulded, artificially, into a community rather than that we are persons made to know our fullness in the Body of Christ of which we are already members. We understand community as something apart from ourselves, a desirable spiritual, social or psychological good, while ignoring the communion written into our being as brothers and sisters in the Elder Brother. It becomes regarded like medicine, intended to correct a fault in our nature, rather than like water, essential because it is a primary constituent of our body.

Communion, then, is a fundamental fact of our existence. It cannot be considered an optional extra, but neither must it be totally identified with its social manifestations. In F. D. Maurice's terms we need to see ourselves as diggers rather than as builders, revealing the communion which exists between us, instead of constructing a community to our own design. Understood from this angle, we can affirm the basic spiritual union already existent in a church and acknowledge its various activities as partial reflections of this greater whole. As with our personal selfhood, we will *be* through the visible community and not identified with it. Too often, however, we approach our church communities as purely social phenomena. Unwittingly, we compare our church with a social club, commitment to which is measured in terms of the number of related activities undertaken. Satisfying for those with the time, energy and freedom to do so, this reinforces, potentially, the loneliness of the housebound sick and elderly, the mother of young children, and the naturally 'unclubbable'. 'I cannot (for whatever reason) attend prayer groups, evening meetings, social gatherings, therefore I do not really belong.' 'I am sick and unable to attend Sunday worship; I do not wish to be a nuisance.'

The reality of our church life at the practical level is, of course, that a relatively small group of people sustain and foster its multiple activities: it is fatally easy to consider them as somehow more members of the Body of Christ than those who, from this viewpoint, let us down by failing to support the Mission, the bazaar, the parish weekend, or who seem to require rather than give help. Viewed from the standpoint of our existing spiritual communion we are able to see that those whose faith is lived out and shared in caring for their families, in involvement in professional and trade associations, in political parties, in simply being for others in their neighbourhood, are equally part of the Body. Those whose lives are a struggle with difficult temperaments, with emotional and psychological distress, are equally enabling the Body to function, their acceptance of their poverty providing its continuing openness to life.

This approach has a powerful counteracting effect on our modern tendency to extreme self-reflectiveness. Rather than congregations being proffered checklists to discern the 'gifts' they can offer to the community, we can be encouraged to understand ourselves and our lives, just as they are, as the initial gift from God and to God, which he will use and make fertile as he will. Instead of thinking in terms of talents, social, physical, psychological, we will be thinking in terms of self-oblation, of being or giving ourselves within the Body. We can then be more imaginative in our unpacking of that image itself, and see just how much its life depends on the hidden factors: the hormones, the chemicals, the inhibitors. No longer do we need to feel constrained to perform a visibly useful function in order to have complete membership of our community. To live fully our own calling, to live as gift rather than as possessor, is to find our place in the Body, whether it is known by all or only by God.

This vision of community does not 'let us off the hook' from promoting and nurturing warm, loving relationships, true Christian friendship; it does suggest, however, that these relationships must be the sign of a wider love, the result of our common acceptance of being loved and joined together by God, and of our union of wills with him. All too often we fall into the temptation of setting out deliberately to engender closeness in the belief that 'God will be in there somewhere' and end by confusing group dynamics with the Holy Spirit. How often do we see people 'crashing' after a small group experience in which relatively transient feelings of togetherness have seemed to offer an awareness of 'love' unknown in the community from which they came? As with any 'mystical' intuition, the proof of the pudding is in the eating: what is of God endures and upholds, what is simply of ourselves evaporates quickly, and before evaporating, produces discontent and impatience with others. Just as in our personal lives, ego apes self and lulls us into believing that because what we have produced is gratifying, it is of God.

My own parish, in recent discussion of our model for church and parish, came up, not surprisingly, with the image of the circle, approved for the equality, interdependence and face-to-face nature of the relationships within it. Quickly the psychological drawbacks of this were perceived. Wonderful to belong to, it is less than wonderful from the outside. In it there is no obvious point of entry, no indication of any openness to, or need of, what lies beyond itself. This is true also on the spiritual level.

When we looked at selfhood and its characteristics we saw that among them were brokenness and incompleteness: the self seeks its perfection, its 'finishing' in God and is therefore open-ended to him and to others. Our model for a community of selves must reflect, on the larger scale, what is true of the person: our community, too, must know its broken-open condition, its unfinished state. As a human community we do not exist apart from our response to the call of God: our *raison d'être* is beyond ourselves. As a human community we are not, and cannot be, complete in ourselves; we cannot, of ourselves, meet all our needs, heal all our wounds: we are gathered together as a people which knows that its sustenance and healing comes from without, that the Body of Christ on earth is truly a broken one. If we ask our communities to be these comforting, enclosing circles in which we are 'fulfilled', where we no longer need know loneliness and that nameless emptiness of hungering for God, then we are asking them to become idols, substitutes for God. The Christian community must be able to support its members through the kind of loving relationship which protects and deepens the longing for God, which develops our discomfiting awareness of our lack of him, of our restlessness, as St Augustine says, until we rest and know fulfilment in him.

Related to this is the question of the orientation of the circle's membership. To maintain desired contact, their direction must always be inward. It may be argued that this is acceptable, for God is at the centre. However, we find with the community the same paradox as with the self: to go inwards, truly, is to be opened out, turned inside-out; the true centre is not within at all. God is found within only to lead us out beyond ourselves. For the glory of the Lord within our communities to be let out, like the self the circle of the community must be broken open to the greater glory beyond us which beckons us on to meet it. The circle cannot, indeed, move anywhere, except around and around itself. In order to move onwards towards the goal, to journey towards the end-time of God's being all in all, the one perfection which matters, we must be side by side facing, not one another, but the God in whom our corporate identity is hidden.

The 'pilgrim people' is here an image come into its own; our communities are of people of no fixed abode but a sure sense of their destination. Called by God for his purpose and not ours we are together not primarily to ensure that we feel secure, comfortable and involved, with a niche in our little social world; fundamentally our visible, tangible togetherness exists to support and encourage one another on a long and

91

arduous journey, undertaken on behalf of all, in which the end-point seems ever to recede.

So far we have been thinking about what a Christian community is for itself. Yet, of course, just like our personal selfhood in the image of Christ, his Body lives by being given away. As this Body, no less than as persons, we are fulfilled only when we are in fact what we have been made to be: bread, broken and distributed to others, leaven, lost in the dough. Jean Vanier has pointed out that Jesus gives two, seemingly contradictory, calls to us: 'Come here to me' and 'Go away'. 'Come to me, all who are heavily burdened' is balanced by 'Go out into the whole world'. We come together to worship and to witness to the transcendent God among us. So often we want to stay there, safe, while Jesus is saying 'Get lost!' 'Go into the "foreign land" of your secularized societies and be used up for me there.' Much of our corporate activity risks leading us into the temptation experienced by the Israelites in the desert, of gathering for ourselves more manna than is needed for the day, ignoring our own vocation as bread. We are tempted to collect ourselves, to possess our group identity as security for tomorrow. If we understand our communities as composed of hungry people called upon to be bread for the world, then we will be able to maintain the balance between grouping and dispersing. We will gather to be fed and scatter to be food for others, to be Jesus in our world.

Our vision of our own nature and that of our community has an importance far beyond our own identity; it governs everything about our relationship to the life of the world. If we understand ourselves as sons and brothers; if we see our baptism as giving new life to that damaged, distorted childship we have through our creation in the image and likeness of God, then we cannot live in indifference to political affairs or with our faith and our politics in separate, discrete boxes. If we truly believe that sonship and brotherhood constitute our very being then working towards the increasing actualization of this reality should be as necessary to us as breathing. The nurturing of brotherhood in our world rests as our particular responsibility, gifted as we are with the fullness of childship and called to be on behalf of others.

Opposition to whatever distorts or denies it is simply part of our rejection of sin.

'Social sin' or 'structural sin' is a term we are accustomed to hearing only in the context of liberation theology, and thus to associating with Marxist insights. Approached, however, from our understanding of selfhood we can see how it is possible to develop a concept of structural sin entirely from within our Christian tradition. Social sin is ego-writ-large, ego built into our social institutions of government, business, crime, family and social life. Our own ego seeks supremacy, autonomy and distinctiveness on our own terms; envisages life as a struggle for scarce resources, a competition in which we must enhance the personality by 'scoring over' others; interprets itself as a possessor and a consumer of a world existing for its benefit. A society living according to such beliefs is, inevitably, 'living in sin': the only possible position for a Christian is as a dissident. As brothers and sisters we all bear some moral guilt for colluding with economic and social systems which destroy the bonds inherent in our nature.

In our modern western world we are trapped in a sterile conflict between two equally ego-based models of Man in society: the individualistic and the collective. The Christian must be like the Irish farmer who opened this discussion and say plainly that neither model can be our starting-point for the development of a sane society, a sane world.

Human beings are made for social living, in a community which affirms their 'dues and duties' – what they can rightly expect as brothers and sisters and what they must give as such. The individualistic model of Man currently in the ascendant strikes at the root of our nature, denying the derived and related condition which is our essence, and encouraging the idolatry of ego. Individualism presupposes the unreality of society as a mere accidental phenomenon in the life of individuals and families. Co-operation is seen as motivated only by self-interest, that is, by the desire to advance or protect the ego's myths about its origins and status. Competition is therefore prized as the means of ensuring individual enhancement, any advantages to wider social life being merely incidental. While superficially it appears to set a high value on the individual person, closer examination reveals just how low an estimation of the human race forms the basis of this model. Humankind is judged here as ego only, as animals incapable of response to spirit, able to be motivated only by the urge to ego-aggrandizement. Brotherhood is denied, capacity for self-transcendence is mocked, and self-sacrifice interpreted as a lunacy resulting from failure in the 'real' world where self-betterment is the goal.

If we believe in the reality of our sonship and brotherhood we will have no option but to reject a model which sets the individual at the centre of our social structure. We will find ourselves inevitably agreeing with the followers of F. D. Maurice that a social system based upon such a vision of dominant ego travesties human beings and travesties the God in whose image they are created. Affirming our selfhood will involve us in repeating their message to their own Victorian age:

> To pretend that any society can ever be *founded* upon competition is about as fearful a mockery as to say that a tortured wretch rests upon the stake that impales him.

People were made to be co-operators, co-workers, with God and with their fellows. It is the power of our inner Cain, the murderer of brotherhood, which persuades us otherwise.

This is not to claim, of course, as left-wing socialists would, that any kind of contest is wrong and that little Susie may not run in the egg-and-spoon race. Trying oneself out against others and against oneself is part of psychological growth. We need to be challenged, in all kinds of ways, to reach beyond what we know of our capacities. What is fundamentally opposed to our vision of self is the establishing of competition at the heart, literally, of social life, as its energy-source. Little Susie's race comes as a small part in her life in which co-operation figures largely, and the experience of competing is not set within an overall context of conflict. The greatest danger with our current polarization between competition and co-operation is that it fails to internalize the former, maintaining it as a 'war of all against all'.

Brotherhood, as we have already seen, does not mean sameness, a merging into the mass which leaves no room for particularity. 'Dreary collectivism' is a term frequently bandied about in political debate and it is, sadly, true. A collectivism which sees the good of the whole as independent of the persons who comprise it offers us no hope, no light; it is as destructive of brotherhood, as unresponsive to spirit, as individualism. The collectivist approach to brotherhood confuses equality of value, equality of being with sameness in terms of personhood. It does not truly reject ego but establishes a mass ego in its place: the social group, rather than the individual, becomes the self-created, self-sustaining entity, identifying its life-source and life-force with its aggregated gifts and predilections, as we see clearly in the rhetoric of any kind of nationalism. Its corresponding vision of God is of the undifferentiated One in whom all individuals are lost, existing only as bits of the whole.

We know God, on the contrary, as Trinity, responding distinctively to Father, Son and Spirit; we know that he, in turn, calls us by name, treats each of us as unique, creates each of us to reflect him in our way and no other. The same is asked of us, so that we work towards a form of social organization which does not prescribe one way of life, one kind of success for all and does not use individual persons as weapons in the struggle of one group against another. For the collectivist, in practice, brotherhood is not an inherent bonding force within humanity; rather is it a socially-developed phenomenon uniting one group sharing their particular conditions in their struggle with another. The intention is not to discern and actualize spiritual realities but to ensure the precedence of one 'corporate ego' over another. Although frequently well-meaning, this is simply one more parody by ego of the reality of human selfhood and human bonding. Despite appearances to the contrary, the collectivist vision of Man in society is still based upon a conflict-model, of egos competing for scarce resources, in which the person is of small worth.

I experienced this, painfully, as a student social worker asked to be involved with a family which had been encouraged to go on a rent-strike. Acknowledged as a useless gesture in itself, it was urged upon them as an attack upon irresponsible landlords. They agreed, in the spirit of true brotherhood which had made their home the hub of the local community. Generous, open people, they were also very vulnerable, stretched by the many demands of a large family and a small income, and psychologically finely-balanced. Of the level of distress, anxiety and dissension generated in the family the initiating community-workers were blissfully unaware; this lovely family were sparrows who did not count, readily replaced in the next round of battle. The language of brotherhood here masked the exploitation of persons, the abnegation of true belonging one to another. I do not see how the Christian can find common ground with this socialist view of brotherhood in class struggle, or, as it is now more commonly phrased, in the struggle of 'the people'.

Christians must be committed to the effort for justice but the 'option for the poor' asked of us cannot, must not, involve identifying the rich and the oppressors as aliens, as non-brothers. Rather, it must invite us to see in them lost sons and brothers, spiritually poor people for whom Jesus longs as much as he delights in those who are poor in him. It urges us to know our oneness with them in our own desires for comfort, security, power and influence in whatever shape or form. We cannot affirm the dignity of each person as a child of God while, in the name of solidarity with the poor, consigning the rest of humanity to spiritual non-existence. In our present popular approach to liberation theology we hover at times dangerously on the brink. The 'goodies', the poor people of God, are ranged in battle against the 'baddies', the multi-nationals, the exploiters of child-labour, totalitarian governments. I have no brief for them, and my instinctive responses to their behaviour are sure proof of my kinship with them. The gospel cuts across these gut reactions and across all our simplistic divisions. God is for sinners; Jesus came to 'become sin', to take the most depraved and degenerate of us home to the Father. We would prefer to sanitize this by extolling 'the poor' over against all others and so minimize the scandal, the truly radical nature of the gospel. In the story of Zacchaeus Jesus' option for the poor was exercised by choosing table-fellowship with the criminal, with the oppressor of the people. Our common way of thinking and choosing seems always to be 'either–or'; God's, by contrast, is 'both–and', both the '*anawim*' and the debased poor man, both John the devoted disciple and Paul the converted persecutor. We, too, are called

to seek justice in ways which acknowledge our solidarity in
sin as well as our solidarity with the oppressed; to look for
solutions which recall all to the life of fellowship. We can only
do this if we balance the notion of 'the people', with its secular
collectivist connotations, with the centrality of God. Our
identity as a human race, as nations, as 'peoples', derives not
from ourselves but from God, who is for all.

This was Charles Kingsley's vision of brotherhood in his
novel *Alton Locke*, where he implicitly contrasts the struggle
for workers' rights in the secular Chartist Movement and in
his own Christian Socialist Movement:

> You are free; God has made you free. You are equals – you
> are brothers; for he is your King, who is no respecter of
> persons. He is your King, to whom all power is given in
> heaven and earth; who reigns and will reign, till he has put
> all enemies under his feet. That was Luther's charter . . .
> That is your charter and mine; the everlasting ground of
> our rights, our mights, our duties . . . Own no other. Claim
> your investiture as free men from none but God!

Kingsley feared that the brotherhood apprehended by
working-men in the Chartist Movement was but a parody of
Christian fraternity, a union of one interest-group against
another. Times and circumstances have changed but what he
perceived as a dangerous distortion in our political and
religious thinking remains equally a threat to us, over one
hundred years later.

8

Icon or idol? – the self in marriage and at work

'Your maker is your husband' (Isaiah 54:5)

'Take the Holy Family as your model.' This was the kind of advice Catholics of the past were accustomed to hearing, advice I remember treating with some scorn as a questioning, unsettled teenager: 'Some family! Husband and wife who have no sexual relationship, father who is not a father, child who is presented as separate from, and superior to, them both. What on earth have they to do with us?' There was, indeed, some truth in this. The Catholic Church, especially, has been guilty of shying away from the enfleshed reality of the life of Jesus and his saints in every aspect other than suffering. Following the example of the family of Nazareth as we had had it presented to us in popular piety seemed to be a sure way of refusing our humanity.

Behind this plaster image, however, I have since discovered valuable insights into the life of the family and its relationship to the outside world which give new force and new meaning to the old exhortation.

Our present model of the family is essentially individualistic. Society is understood as being comprised of families much as a wall is composed of individual bricks: their interdependence is a matter of choice and their cohesion relies upon the externally-applied mortar of convention and necessity. The life of the family is seen to be affected by social changes, social attitudes, but is not perceived as intrinsically part of that larger society. Families, like individuals, belong to themselves, with no necessary bonds to others. In other words, the family is approached as a larger-scale ego. Ties are acknowledged and embraced within the family unit but extend no further; concepts of derivation, relationship and sacrifice, where accepted, are considered to apply only within the tight family circle. Parents may 'sacrifice' themselves in tireless effort to provide material security and desirable experiences for their children; children may recognize with thankfulness what is offered them in love and respond in kind. But all too often the love stops here, becoming a form of love of ego; we give to ourselves in our families in an endless circularity which deprives others of time, attention, money, energy. The needs of family members are not so much met as overmet, as it were: the neglect of family life upon 'conversion' which Père Grou reproved is frequently found in reverse today. We are, indeed, in constant danger of living the dictum 'Christianity is a religion of the family' as a literal truth; the family all too frequently becomes for us not the means of living out our faith but its focus and end-point, its God. The family is seen as existing to and for itself, as a need-filling, aspiration-filling organism: like the ego it looks inwards upon itself as sustainer, source and purpose of its own existence. Rather than enabling its members to share the love experienced within it, it consumes them, demanding living sacrifice.

We need to be aware of this potential, especially today when so much emphasis is laid upon the importance of family life by the Government, the manufacturing and advertising industries, and the Churches. In a largely deChristianized society like ours, being vaguely Christian is often summed up as 'I do not do anybody any harm', as a mild wash of virtue over our social behaviour and conventions, which makes the family a 'good thing', without further analysis. How easy it is for us as Christians, then, to seize on this as common ground and, as we survey soaring divorce rates and the statistics on broken families, to urge a simplistic return to the old values of family meals, family prayers, family churchgoing, without asking: 'What kind of family do we want to reinforce?' It is here that I think the old exhortation 'look at the Holy Family' may truly come into its own.

Today we all believe, so it seems, that marriage is primarily for 'the fostering of mutual love'. So far so good. In practice I suspect most of us interpret this as meaning that the couple have come together 'to make each other happy', to fulfil the other's personality. In this way the partners look inwards upon one another, forming an ego-as-couple. Children are the further expression of this reciprocal fulfilment, widening the circle. Still the direction is inwards towards the life of the pair which is to be 'completed' by the arrival of children.

If we look at Mary and Joseph, taking the biblical story at face value, as did our hagiographers, what a different picture emerges. At the centre of their relationship is a divine call, a task to be fulfilled, in which their mutual love is for sustenance and support: together they respond to God's will; together they look beyond their own partnership, to God. Their marriage is truly a vocation which opens them up to life.

Their common task is the rearing of a child who is to be a mystery and a source of pain to them. This child cannot be possessed. When Mary is the naturally anxious mother, she is reminded of the priority: Jesus must look beyond them as parents, to his Father. The family unit is not allowed to exist as its own purpose; the child does not live for the parents, while their living for him must not be allowed to tie him to them. The pain of their possible loss of their son at twelve years old is part of this family's fundamental broken-open state. It must not seek security in the comfortable feeling of exclusive belonging to one another.

This brokenness increases for Mary, who is never permitted to rest in the pleasure of motherhood at the natural level. She has to see her son negate this and reinterpret it as a motherhood originating in faith, in the acceptance of her 'daughterhood' to God in receiving and keeping his word. Mary has to die to her exclusive claims on Jesus and receive him again as one member of the human family. In his death her motherhood is again restyled and broken open to extend to all Jesus' followers, to all who are restored in him: 'Woman, this is your son' (John 19:27). Mary is not allowed to hold on to her status as mother as though it were a possession, giving her rights over the child and expectations of him, which would enable her to feel 'fulfilled' in and through his success, or to act the tragic heroine in his defeat. When one aspect of her task of motherhood closes in a way excruciating to every natural feeling, she is asked to start again in a new dimension.

Mary has to abandon every scrap of the desire to cling to her motherhood 'in the flesh', to possess Jesus with that overwhelming protective love mothers feel for their children, not so that she can become indifferent to it but so that it can be expanded to a deeper, broader awareness of family, of motherhood, 'childship' and brotherhood in God.

Of Joseph we know next to nothing apart from his constancy in protecting child and mother in obedience to God. Coming from cultures placing so much value on patrimony, is not such silence remarkable? All that the gospel writers feel we need to know about this father, this husband, is encapsulated here in the fulfilment, not of his own or his wife's needs, but of God's call.

It is easy to see the difference between our two models of family life. The first looks to itself for its sustenance and purpose: its relationship with other families, other persons is incidental to its life. We might call it parodic of the love within the Trinity: it is given, received and returned without that overflow, that ecstasy or going beyond oneself, which characterizes our Trinitarian God. When established as an ideal, this kind of family-living becomes an idol, a travesty of divine truth. On the other hand we can see our 'Holy Family' as truly holy, as an icon of the ecstatic love of the Blessed Trinity, of persons in communion turned outwards towards God and others.

If we take *this* family as our model, because it is an imaging of God's truth, we will, indeed, be able to discern the kind of family and married life we desire for our society. We will promote an ideal of the family close to that of the monastic community, 'a school of the Lord's service', a preparation for a wider apprehension of relationships and duties, as George MacDonald taught in *Unspoken Sermons*:

Why does my brother come of the same mother and father? Why do I behold the helplessness of his infancy? . . . I have had the sons of my mother that I may learn the universal brotherhood. For there is a bond between me and the most wretched liar that ever died for the murder he would not confess, closer infinitely than that which springs only from having the one mother and father. That we are the sons

101

and daughters of God . . . is a bond closer than all other
bonds in one.

This pattern of family life is, I am convinced, not only
spiritually but also psychologically healthy, for it allows for
respect and space for each person within it and opposes the
development of false expectations of its members. We shall
look first at the marital relationship.

The biblical picture of marriage, as we have seen, is rooted
in the idea of response to God's call and purposes: Mary and
Joseph, but also Abraham and Sarah, Jacob and Rachel,
Joseph and Rebecca. Marriage unites a couple for a life-giving
end far transcending the attainment of personal happiness.
But God's call to persons is in itself metaphorical, in biblical
terms, of his call to a people. Marriage is a basic way in which
God's relationship with humankind could be represented. In
Isaiah, in Hosea, Israel is the bride: this, of course, culminates
in St Paul's view of marriage as sign of the relationship
between Christ and the Church, God and his people. But in
marriage the two 'become one flesh': marriage as sign of the
relationship between Jesus and his Church is also sign of the
incarnation, of the two-into-one of God's assumption of our
humanity. There is a sense, then, in which marriage is symbolic of the essential identity of the self as a created, enfleshed,
image of God. Our selfhood results from the nuptial union of
Christ with the humanity in which we share. In one's self,
therefore, whether married or single, we are in this way
'wedded': 'your maker is your husband' (Isaiah 54:5) applies
to each of us in our depths. The 'mystical marriage' apprehended by some great mystics is not really a future state to be
enjoyed only by a few, but our prior, true identity, left imperfectly realized by most of us. The self's most basic apprehension of union is of union with God, scarcely actualized, but
the root of our life. As Julian of Norwich said, God is always
with us although we may be rarely with him.

The marriage relationship, then, must not be allowed to
replace this apprehension of weddedness, but must protect it,
nurturing its growth. Like the members of religious communities, married couples need to be the first defenders of the
space and uniqueness of one another and of the loneliness for

God, the singleness for him, which is our experience of 'the already and the not yet'. If one's true, as yet unactualized self, is 'wedded', is united by grace to God, then our here-and-now experience is of unfulfilment, of longing and yearning for the courts of the Lord (Psalm 84). Each of us will be 'single' not only in being single-minded, but also in the sense of having been made for another, of being left incomplete.

This state is the other, fundamental, base for our experience of personhood, but all too often we interpret it in psychological terms only, especially when it has hooked up from the past memories of loneliness and has become overlaid with the pain of present failures and failings in relationships. When we do so, how easily the total condition is labelled 'bad' and 'destructive', how readily is marriage looked to as the remedy. The spouse is then subconsciously expected to be God for his or her partner, filling up all awareness of loneliness, emptiness, dissatisfaction. I well remember the sickening shock of discovering just how lonely marriage could be and of beginning to question, as a result, the basis for the relationship. Since then I have known many people similarly affected. Prepared to meet difficulties and disagreements, to accept 'for worse' as well as 'for better', they had nevertheless anticipated, implicitly, that marriage would root out their fundamental feelings of lostness and loneliness.

It is not surprising, therefore, that marriages fail when couples are asked to carry the burden of responsibility for each other's existential security and satisfaction. When partners live in such an unreal world, idolizing their spouses as all-supplying gods, they have few resources, spiritual or emotional, to meet difficult patches. If one's idol is proved to have clay feet, the great temptation is to refashion another; are not multiple serial marriages evidence of this pursuit within another of what no person can provide? Alternatively, how attractive it is to dispense with all gods whatsoever, real or imagined, once one has failed to fulfil the fantasy, and to reject all relationships as worthless or oppressive.

Once again so much pain and disorder erupts into our social life from this conversion of an icon into an idol. The love-relationship intended as a sign of the love between God and humankind, of the union between heaven and earth, becomes a parodic relationship in which the created mimics the Creator. We make the same mistake with our marriage as we do with our bodies, our personalities, our communities: we identify ourselves with our married status, as something in itself, rather than accepting it as our way of being in the world: 'I *am* through my marriage.' Through the day-to-day living in union with another I grow in the experience of loving as willing (perhaps I do not always feel loving when I get up in the night to make hot drinks for my husband, but I do wish for his relief from pain). I also find this life-in-partnership reverberating spiritually, making me more aware of that other union even more basic to my existence. Just as my week spent in prayer before the Taizé icon of mother and child produced in me first psychological and then spiritual recognition, so a lifetime of *living* the icon, marriage, produces similar recognition, without in any way denying the solidity and validity of the human bonding.

Once we grasp that this is part of our vocation as married people, and that we are 'lost in the land of unlikeness', we become free from making impossible demands and we allow the mystery of the other person full scope. We no longer expect of ourselves perfect, godlike knowledge of our partner and from him or her the delivery of all the secrets of their being to be our possession. We will be able to prevent the rightful necessity of sharing, of intuitive knowledge between partners tipping into a denial of the hiddenness of our selfhood. Rather, we will treasure the secret of our spouse's identity, knowing it is safe within the God who has called us together.

What is true of marriage is equally true of our relationship with our children. I have already suggested that in our society children are regarded as subsidiary to a marriage, coming into being to 'complete' a marriage, to meet parents' needs. All too often parenthood is now regarded as an automatic right to be exercised solely at will. Procreation is no longer regarded as participation in a mystery which transcends us. Now it should be subjected to our will, manipulable for the fulfilment of our desires. The act of creation is assumed to be ours and the resulting children consequently our possessions. This struck me forcibly upon the birth of our daughter.

Everyone congratulated my husband and me in ways which suggested she was our product. We were being encouraged to pin a placard, 'All our own work', on her and bask in the glory of the artist. It was hard work to make many people understand that I could nowhere find such pride: the child was entirely gift. The joy I felt in her derived totally from amazement at her existence and her beauty. As with my selfhood in the experience of 'light' in earlier years, I felt she was of me but not mine. Possibly my experience of needing drugs both to conceive and to maintain a pregnancy contributed to this: I could scarcely feel my husband and I had been independent creators. Certainly the whole problem of infertility had raised for me, painfully, the question of idolatry within the family. It became clear that the desire for a child, initially a response to, and expression of, God's life-giving love was constantly in danger of becoming a desire to fill myself up, to have a clear purpose and status in life; it could easily slip into a means of ceasing to know my life as a never completely answered question by providing a flesh-and-blood reason for living. The urge to be a co-operator, a pro-creator, with God, could all too readily become a pressure to fulfil ego, to turn inwards from God to a vision of ego-as-mother, source, sustainer.

Our capacity to manipulate nature and to 'correct' infertility is double-edged. So often it enables the triumph of ego in doctor and patient alike, as they join in flight from the pain of childlessness. I am convinced that if we can see ourselves, and therefore our children, as pure gift, we can, however much it may also hurt, see infertility as a gift. We can see it not as God's denial to us of the grace of parenthood but as his invitation to discover and reveal our role as co-creators with him, within the total human family. Understood in this way we can endure the pain of infertility without denying its searching intensity and yet know ourselves to be like the barren woman who will be the mother (or father) of many children. This is hard to take. I believed it when I thought a child of our own was not a possibility. I repeat it to myself when I am tempted to envy or shame at the sight of 'proper' families of more than one child. Parenthood and our failure in its physical expression should be a call to a deeper poverty, a deeper awareness of God as our source and as the One whose parental love we feebly reflect. How quick we are to turn our children into our wealth and our childlessness into a protest against our injured proprietorial rights!

This possessiveness of our children, together with our inadequate understanding of relationships within the body, may prove destructive of them, psychologically as well as spiritually. Because we believe children are ours and because we feel that they are 'flesh of our flesh', we tend to conceive of the family as one unit into which all the children are merged as a body, with the parents at the head, controlling all, knowing all. This tendency to parody the headship of Christ in the Body is, I am sure, inherent in our popular vision of family life. Its destructiveness can best be seen by considering it at its worst, in the family with an anorectic member.

In most cases, a person with anorexia nervosa is not so much a sick person, but the symptom of a sick family which has a distorted and extreme view of family life, developed perhaps over generations in response to psychological distress and deprivation, and to a misunderstanding of the nature of personal existence.

Such families are usually keenly aware of their kinship bonds: parents value highly family activities such as family meals as symbols of family unity. They tend, however, rarely to extend their awareness of bonds outwards. The family circle is tight, developing, as it were, a firm boundary around the corporate ego of the family. Children are valued, unwittingly, as extensions of the parental ego: understood as expressions of the parents' identity, they are therefore not allowed to reveal, or even experience, feelings, wishes, aspirations which lie beyond the scope of the parents and threaten with their difference. The parents believe that, to be the good parents they must prove themselves to be, they should know everything about their children and meet all their needs. They have not separated themselves from their children and cannot consider their parenthood in anything other than biological terms. They must feed, clothe and protect their offspring: any attempt of the child's to autonomy and independence in these areas seems a threat to their role and must be denied. The emergence of other, less tangible or visible needs, further frightens the parents, and appears as a challenge to their adequacy and godlike knowledge of their children. Once more the only available strategy is denial: our children only want and need what we are able to provide. Hence the children's growing sense of psychological separateness and autonomy is violated; their burgeoning sense of integrity is reinterpreted for them as wicked rebelliousness and their needs as totally unacceptable, 'bad' feelings which must be suppressed. Ultimately the children themselves thus become locked into the parents' fantasy of being their creation. The parents, especially the mother, are the repository for each child's identity; they, and they alone, truly know the children's needs, desires, abilities. When the parents are pleased with the children, they are good and happy; when the parents are in a bad mood, the children are damnable.

In this kind of family, food normally takes an important role, symbolic of the parents', and particularly the mother's, need to feel the perfect provider. For the child to be fed is in fact to feed the mother with assurance of her capacity to satisfy her children. For a child to exercise choice by refusing food or to express a preference is experienced as a denial of the mother's adequacy and cannot be allowed. Eating then becomes a battle, a war of independence. For the child (now, usually teenager, and usually female) refusal to eat is double-edged. At one level it is the one means of affirming separateness: 'No longer will I swallow all you give me', meaning not only food, but ideas about one's identity, one's worth, one's world. At another level it is self-punishment for harbouring all those unacknowledged needs which have been labelled 'bad'. Constantly to be told 'You are never satisfied', in response to any expression of needs or aspirations not countenanced by the parents or to any failure in gratitude for what is bestowed results in a deep shame at existing as such a needy being and at being a 'nuisance' for daring to be alive in any kind of particularity. Ultimately to exist at all feels like committing an offence: starving is a means of minimizing this offence and at the same time of becoming outwardly an image of the anorectic's inner being, starved of the integrity and particularity due to him or her.

Generally all the family members are involved in the

maintenance of its myth of perfection and normality. The anorectic child is usually one who has always been 'difficult' and 'different', with needs and temperament more challenging to the parents' pretensions, or from whom there has been the most resistance to separation. Anorectics are thus marked out for special treatment by their siblings, who use them to soak up their aggression and their negativity and to exercise upon them their otherwise thwarted ability to control, while maintaining equilibrium within the family unit.

The psychological (and physical) harm caused by such a pattern of family life is evident. What is less obvious is the immense spiritual problem met by sufferers from anorexia in trying to rescue from this wide-ranging experience of denial any true apprehension of selfhood, since so much of what they have known travesties the concept of the spiritual self.

Any anorexia sufferers would probably find no difficulty in accepting that their selfhood is found in God rather than in themselves, since at the psychological level God has been their parents. However, such acknowledgement would be accompanied by terror, by panic: all their efforts have so far been directed at retrieving some control, at being no longer dependent upon the will and whim of another. The need of trust in the constant, reliable love of God, in whom their selfhood is secure, is an almost overwhelming obstacle to someone whose sense of personal acceptability has hung for so long upon the changing moods of parents. The concept of the self as gift likewise arouses boundless anxiety: their experience of receiving has been one of humiliation and of uncertainty, for the gift may always be recalled. Allowing oneself to be open to God is a similar source of terror, for there has already been an experience of being taken over and 'filled up' as an annihilation of particularity. In other ways, too, anorectics have encountered parodic versions of selfhood. The self-renouncing self is familiar to them, for they have long since learnt that they are only justified in existing when gratifying the desires of others: to be manipulable to the needs of others is a mere fact of existence. The weakness of their own sense of identity lends itself to discernment of spiritual bonding, but this, too, has been known only in its tyrannical form as the family octopus, whose tentacles stifle with

demands for family loyalty and duty any attempt to counter-
act its myth and destroy its idol. God in himself is known as
a persecuting void, for where true sustenance has been sought
there has been found only its parody in the assurance-seeking
giving of the family, leaving a sense of emptiness and betrayal.

What the anorexia sufferer undergoes to an extreme degree
is, I am convinced, but a heightened experience of the more
hidden dynamics of our modern family life, dynamics
reinforced, rather than countered, by our dominant vision of
the self and its relationships. I have examined this condition
in depth because it proves to us so forcefully that our understanding of our personhood is of immense practical importance. Not simply an interesting subject for those of us with a
theological bent, it is essential for our approach to any
renewal of family life and for any properly God-centred, spiritually sensitive pastoral counselling. A restored doctrine of
the human person is no immediate panacea for all our social
and psychological ills, but it does offer us a new model for
personal and family living, a base from which to develop new
ways of relating in families, ways resistant to the expectations
and demands long sanctified by our ego-dominated culture.

More often than not our present emphasis in social and
church life upon support for family life leaves single people
feeling insignificant, unwanted, even something of an aber-
ration. Socially they are considered to have the material
means and the freedom to 'enjoy life'; politically, their lack
of dependants ensures that they are at the bottom of the heap
when it comes to welfare rights and provision. In their local
church they are frequently made to feel an irrelevance amid
the family-oriented services, mothers and toddlers groups,
young wives groups and so on, or are regarded as an
inexhaustible supply of labour. Single people are expected to
be more available than their married peers, who may easily
fall into an exploiting relationship with them.

A renewed grasp of our spiritual bonds, of the reality of
our brotherhood and of the true nature of the family gives us
a firm foundation from which to work to change social and
political attitudes. Within the Church, our understanding of
the self as 'wedded' has much to say about the identity and

the vocation of single people and about their relationship to married Christians.

If we take seriously the belief that marriage is 'an outward sign of the inward grace' of God's union with our humanity then we can see that it is not a grace limited to its bearers. Married people specialize, as it were, as an icon of God's love in the incarnation, speaking of the truth about us all, while living it in a particularized way. Single people need to be enabled to see in those who are married not pairs living an entirely different sort of life but reminders of the inner union which they are called to recover. Their singleness, whether chosen or not, is to be seen as a sign of our incompleteness, our loneliness for God, which is found also in married partners. Each of us, then, married or single, finds the complementary state both within ourselves and mirrored in others.

Availability, therefore, is not the justification for singleness nor its major attribute. Similarly parenthood, the nurturing of life, is not the province solely of the married. To fulfil their calling parents have to learn to let go of their physical parenthood, not only in letting their children go but in opening up their awakened capacity for nurturing to others, children or not. To be truly fruitful their love must make them more fully available to others: true lovers look outwards in love for all they see. Single people need to discover in their union with God the creativity and nurturing ability which is theirs because it is his. All of us, in becoming full selves, must know the spiritual maternity of which Guerric of Igny has spoken. Such maternity does not end with ourselves but makes of us also spiritual midwives to our brothers and sisters.

That very different and very difficult challenges confront single people and married couples today I do not, in any way, deny. Neither would I wish to ignore the differing demands of the two ways of life. I am suggesting, however, that there is more in common between them than we frequently acknowledge and that many of our current problems are exacerbated by our tendency to set the one against the other. Because we have lost the notion of brotherhood and have had no conceptual tools for discerning spiritual likeness, we tend to note only that what separates and divides us. The single person resents paying for the services which benefit children;

the married couple regard the single homeless as simply feckless and able to look after themselves. The lonely single person frets with envy at the sight of married people and leaps into a disastrous marriage; the harassed working mother alienates her husband and children with her burning resentment at the restrictions on her freedom and longs for the liberation of the single bedsit. A vision of selfhood which enables us to unite within ourselves the paradox of weddedness and singleness can free us to overcome our envy and our fantasies about the life of others. It can free us from that sterile either–or approach to social organization, whether it be at the political level, within our local communities or within our churches.

That other potential icon or idol in our modern society is, of course, work. From the Christian viewpoint there are two complementary aspects to the idea of work. In the early chapters of Genesis the necessity of work, of labouring to provide for ourselves, results from the Fall. Man in his rupture from God has broken the bonds with the earth which would have provided his needs. Working, therefore, reminds Man of his contingency; he is not the master of creation; unlike God, he cannot simply speak and have it done. To run away from a life involving some element of labour is therefore to run away from the reality of our nature as created beings who are out of harmony with the world for which they were made.

In her rule for her sisters St Clare wrote of 'the grace of working'. The necessity of work has not only its penitential aspect, as a repairer of our pride, it is also, through Christ, a gift conveying dignity to the recipient. Work draws us closer to the God who in the incarnation became a craftsman. Not an end in itself, our work is one means of becoming like God, one means of knowing ourselves as co-workers with God in the unfolding of a creation which involves us within it. Fulfilment is thus realized through, and not in, work. Lived in this way man the worker is an icon of God the creator, the collaborator (the co-labourer) pointing towards its uncreated source.

How much this differs from our modern western approach! We have made of work, identified only with paid employment, an idol which consumes us while being expected to fulfil our needs. In so doing we have totally recoiled from the notion of work as labour, as an activity involving unremitting effort. We bristle with 'labour-saving' devices which 'save time' for 'real' work (which is to be self-fulfilling) or for leisure. Making things as a craft hobby is encouraged as fulfilling while the work required to keep a home clean is despised as drudgery. I write as one condemned by my own pen. Housework is not one of my favourite occupations but I become increasingly aware of the pride and escapism involved in my evasions. It is so easy to consider writing this book as my 'real work', in which I feel more fully 'myself', and to regard as drudgery to be dispensed with as quickly as possible the work which demands from me the physical exertion I am less inclined to make. Here, being 'fulfilled' by work is synonymous with satisfying the ego, and what does not meet that criterion is dismissed as unworthy of my time. Instead of seeing the not very onerous tasks of cleaning, cooking, washing-up and so on as part and parcel of my existence as a created being (and one which binds me closely with my brothers and sisters for whom daily living *is* onerous), I see it as an imposition, as an unfair demand on my time, a distraction from my true business. Rather than approaching every simple job as a means of glorifying God, a sharing in his work of making order out of chaos, I grade and value the activities according to the satisfaction provided in terms of feeling 'used'. In my intellectual pride I decide which aspects of my daily work are sanctified by God and substitute the preferences of my ego for his will. When I am in this frame of mind no longer is my day a sacrifice of praise to him but an act of homage to my ego.

I suspect I am not alone in this and only wish I had understood it some years ago when working with an elderly man who felt his life had been wasted. In sixty years of employment he had not enjoyed a single day. Work for him had truly been a labour of love, to maintain his family. I would not seek to validate the conditions in which he was employed or the social systems which ill-used his talents; I would like to be able to tell him that what he achieved in the loving giving of himself through his work was far more than can be measured by the yardstick of satisfaction. One of the worst aspects of our present attitude to work is that it does rob of any sense of dignity those people whose work is not experienced as self-expression or does not yield the high rewards of money, power or status. We speak to such an extent about choice of *careers* that the majority of people are denied their honourable status as workers.

Work has also become increasingly identified with paid employment. Labour is only valued when it can be priced (even if as cheaply as possible); consequently workers are only valued when they are paid for their efforts. When I work for the church voluntarily, taking a seminar or leading a parish weekend, to many I am a middle-class housewife indulging herself or, conversely, being exploited. When I am paid for identical activities I acquire rights and status as a fee-earning worker. Work has, therefore, become defined as those activities from which the individual worker obtains tangible benefits rather than those which promote social well-being. Fulfilment through work is seen as the satisfaction of ego rather than the actualization of the self as a being for others and a co-worker with God.

This, for me, is one of the great dilemmas resulting from the Women's Movement. Great emphasis is being placed currently on 'liberating' women, achieving 'justice' for them, by increasing their access to paid employment. To be equal in our western society, it is implied, one must be a money-earning worker (I am tempted to say a wage-slave). Women are not honoured for their work, freely undertaken, in families, communities, charities, churches. Frequently they are belittled as parasites, 'cabbages', Lady Bountifuls – depending on their sphere of activity – while their contribution to the life of their country is ignored. Is the answer simply to enhance women's position within our crazy value-system or to undertake the slower, harder process of challenging it? It seems to me that this is a crucial issue for our churches. In responding penitently to the suppression of women sanctioned and encouraged by past official church attitudes, we are in danger of once more affirming, rather than questioning, prevailing social mores. There is every sign of a succumbing to a secular version of liberation which binds women to an idolatrous model of work and a debased vision of the person as a bought-and-sold worker. In so doing we would be validating the model, equally, for men, furthering thus the growth of a society whose one basis for relationship is the cash-nexus, a society fit only for Cain.

I have deliberately written so far about fulfilment through work, seeing it as a means to an end of either self-fulfilment or ego-gratification. Today, however, work has become for many an end in itself and a substitute for personal identity. Increasingly we see people submerging themselves in their work. On the pretext of slaving to support their families (and increase their possession of consumer goods) they sacrifice time, energy, abilities on the altar of their chosen occupation in order to avoid the realities of their own identity, their loneliness, their incompleteness, their need for relationship. All the questions facing the human person, all the mystery of our being can be evaded by the creation of a self-image as teacher, shopkeeper, businessman, minister. The material rewards and the exhaustion issuing from over-exertion furthermore ensure that there is neither space, inclination nor alertness to confront these in whatever leisure-time remains. Hence the collapse into depression upon sudden redundancy or the decline into ill-health upon retirement, unless the obsessional pursuit of a hobby supplies a new identity: 'I am a golfer' fills the gap left by 'I am an electrician; a plumber; a bank manager'.

Hence, too, the loss of any sense of direction in young people who leave school with no prospect of employment or who, full of hope, find no work. Our social values offer them no other source of dignity and identity but that of employee. Voluntary work is not labelled 'proper work', though it may cost them their state benefits: working is wholly linked with earning a wage.

On the other hand, their own teen culture, developed out of our 'take the waiting out of wanting' ethos, emphasizes immediate gratification. For them, too, self-fulfilment equals ego-satisfaction: 'I enjoy myself therefore I am.' After a time, when the goal of finding work has receded, and some pleasure is derived from hanging about with friends, is it surprising that a tension arises between the adult-proffered model of 'self-as-paid-employee' and their own version of 'self-as-grati-fied-ego'? Adults have conflated these two, while for such young people they are distinct and opposite forces. Since no one has offered them a vision in which unpaid work is valued and ends other than an adult version of ego-satisfaction attainable from working, is it any wonder that they often reject the world of employment for a life on the dole with their friends? They have been offered an idol which has failed them and so have turned to fashioning one for themselves.

God has made us to be his images, sharers in the humanity of the carpenter of Nazareth and in the divinity of a Creator always at work in his creation. He made us to work not for him but with him, as collaborators in the fulfilment of Christ's work of redemption. It has often been remarked that the story of our salvation begins in a garden and ends in a city. God calls us to work to fashion the City of God: all our life of fast from ego, all that we do to proclaim God as the centre, the model, the end, of humanity, all that we do to realize brotherhood and sacrifice in our society, is part of that work. To be ourselves, as workers, as married couples, as single people we need only root ourselves in him, and make our own those words of St Augustine:

> To the Lord, all. In the Lord, all. God be our hope, God be our fortitude. God be our firmness. He be our prayer, he be our praise. He be the help by which we labour. He be the end in which we rest.

References and further reading

Chapter 1
References to St Irenaeus are from his *Five books against the heresies*, in the Library of Fathers of the Holy Catholic Church 1872. A taste of Irenaeus can be gathered from Henry Bettenson, *The Early Christian Fathers*, OUP 1956. This is a very useful introduction.

The reference to Gerard Manley Hopkins is from his poem 'That nature is a Heraclitean fire and of the comfort of the resurrection'. Do not let the long-winded title put you off trying Hopkins's poems, which are difficult but well worth the effort. Try also his short poem 'As kingfishers catch fire'. His collected works are available in Penguin paperback.

Chapter 2
References to George MacDonald are to his book-length poem *A book of strife, in the form of a diary of an old soul*. As far as I am aware, this is now out of print. His great novel *Lilith* and his children's stories are published by Lion and Scripture Union.

The quotation from St John of the Cross is his 'Prayer of a soul enkindled by love' found in *The Collected Works of St John of the Cross*, ed. and trans. Kieran Kavanagh and Otilio Rodriguez, Institute of Carmelite Studies 1973.

The extract from Guerric of Igny is found in his *Liturgical Sermons*, ed. and trans. Hilary Costello ocso and John Morson ocso, Cistercian Publications 1971.

The reference to F. D. Maurice is found in *The Life of Frederick Denison Maurice, chiefly told in his own letters*, ed. Frederick Maurice, Macmillan 1884. Perhaps the best introductions to Maurice are A. M. Allchin's *The Kingdom of Love and Knowledge*, DLT 1979 and Frank Mauldin McClain's *Maurice, Man and Moralist*, SPCK 1972.

Gregory of Nyssa is most readily available in the compilation by Jean Daniélou SJ, *From Glory to Glory*, St Vladimir Seminary Press 1979.

Chapter 3
The extract from St Francis de Sales is from a letter to St Jane
Frances de Chantal, quoted in E. K. Sanders, *Sainte Chantal*, SPCK
1918. An ideal introduction to St Francis is Michael Hollings's
compilation *Athirst for God*, DLT 1985; a more complex guide is
Wendy M. Wright, *Bond of Perfection*, Paulist Press 1985. I hope
that the Library of Western Spirituality edition of Francis and
Jane's letters will be available in Britain shortly.

The reference to Jean-Nicolas Grou is from his *Spiritual Maxims*,
Burns and Oates 1956, the companion to his *Marks of True Devotion*.

Chapter 4
All references to the community of Pain de Vie (Bread of Life) are
from Pascal and Marie-Annick Pingault, *Fioretti du Pain de Vie*,
Editions Fayard 1985. (Translation mine.)

The closing quotation is from T. S. Eliot's study of conscience
and martyrdom in St Thomas à Becket in *Murder in the Cathedral*,
Faber 1956.

Chapter 6
St Francis de Sales is found in *The Interior Spirit of the Visitation of
Holy Mary*, Baltimore Visitation 1927.

Jean-Pierre de Caussade is found in two translations as *The Sacrament of the Present Moment*, trans. Kitty Muggeridge, Fount 1981 and
Algar Thorold, *Self-abandonment to Divine Providence*, Fontana 1971.
His *Spiritual Letters*, 'Ordeals of souls' and 'Comfort in ordeals', are,
sadly, out of print.

The reference to Walter Hilton comes from his *Scale of Perfection*
(sometimes known as *The Ladder of Perfection*), now out of print in
Britain.